JOHN CAIRNEY, 'The Man Who Played Robert Burns', is an actor, writer, lecturer and football fan.

After National Service 1948-50 Cairney enrolled at the Glasgow College of Drama and the University of Glasgow simultaneously, graduating in drama in 1953. In 1989 he gained an MLitt from Glasgow University for a History of Solo Theatre and in 1994 a PhD from Victoria University, Wellington for his study of R.L. Stevenson and Theatre.

Cairney's professional association with Burns began in 1965 with the one man show, *There was a Man* by Tom Wright. In 1968 he wrote and starred in a six-part serial of the Burns story for Scottish Television, *Burns*. From 1975-79 his company Shanter Productions organised a Burns festival in Ayr. From 1974-81 he toured the world with his solo version of *The Robert Burns Story* and from 1981-85 he toured with his wife, New Zealand actress Alannah OSullivan, in *The Burns Experience*. In 1986 Shanter Productions presented the first full-length modern Burns musical *There Was A Lad*. In 1996 in commemoration of the Burns International Year a video, *Robert Burns: An Immortal Memory*, was issued, written and narrated by Cairney.

Prior to and interspersed between these performances he played a multitude of other characters on stage, radio, television and film. His films include *Jason and the Argonauts, Victim* and *A Night to Remember*. His theatre work includes *Cyrano de Bergerac* at Newcastle; C. S. Lewis in *Shadowlands* at the Court Theatre, Christchurch, as well as *Murder in the Cathedral* and *Macbeth* at the Edinburgh Festival. On television he played the lead in *This Man Craig*, as well as appearing in many other popular series.

Since 1990 Cairney has lived in Auckland, New Zealand. He has written two autobiographies and is still very much in demand as a lecturer, writer and consultant on all aspects of Burns.

By the same author:
The Man Who Played Robert Burns, 1987 (Mainstream)
East End to West End, 1988 (Mainstream)
Worlds Apart, 1991 (Mainstream)
A Scottish Football Hall of Fame, 1998 (Mainstream)

On the Trail of
Robert Burns

JOHN CAIRNEY

Luath Press Limited

EDINBURGH

www.luath.co.uk

First Edition 2000

The paper used in this book is acid-free, neutral-sized and recyclable.
It is made from low chlorine pulps produced in a low energy, low
emission manner from renewable forests.

Printed and bound by
Bell & Bain Ltd., Glasgow

Typeset in 10.5 point Sabon by
S. Fairgrieve, Edinburgh

Maps by Jim Lewis

Illustrations by
Murray Robertson, Historic Illustration, Falkirk

Contents

This book is respectfully dedicated to
that fine Scot and man of the theatre,
DR JIMMY LOGAN OBE FRSAMD
who cast me as Robert Burns in 1959
and started me off on the trail...

Acknowledgements

I AM ESPECIALLY INDEBTED to Dr James Mackay's masterworks on Burns – *Burns*, the biography, the *Complete Works and the Complete Letters* – not to mention, *The Complete Word Finder*, *Burnsiana* and his *History of the Burns Federation*. These books have helped guide my feet over so many familiar, well-trodden paths yet still allowed me my own views and opinions. For the sake of consistency, all Burns quotes used here, whether from poem, song or letter, are from these publications unless otherwise stated. I am also happy to acknowledge the friendship of the learned author over many years. Similarly, another ally has been Dr Maurice Lindsay. His *Burns Encyclopaedia* has been with me as a reference since I started on Burns in 1959 and I couldn't be without it in anything related to the Bard. Still on a personal level, I must mention the assistance given by the work of another learned doctor, Bill Murray, as well as that of a much-missed associate, the late Alan Bold, whose *A Burns Companion* contained *A Burns Topography* which I found quite invaluable. Recourse was also made to James Barke's edition of the works and also those of Professor James Kinsey and Dr Tom Crawford.

I am also grateful to Raymond Lamont Brown's definitive publications on the Burns tours through the Borders and in the Highlands and Stirlingshire as well as particular articles such as *The West Highland Tour* (Allan Bayne) and *Burns as a Tourist* (Andrew McCallum) published in the 1944 edition of the *Burns Chronicle* by the Burns Federation. The *Chronicle* also gave me the opportunity of checking with Dr Duncan McNaught's *Burns Chronology* from 1895. Considerable help has also been given to me by Burnsians over the years such as the late John McVie, Jock Thomson and Jim McCaffrey as well as later contacts like Sam Gaw, Peter Westwood, John Inglis and Tom Paterson.

There are too many assisting individual miscellaneous articles to acknowledge but I must mention all Burns material issued by the Scottish Tourist Board since 1975 and the individual writings of such authorities as Professor David Daiches, Dr Ian Grimble, Neil Gow QC, Gavin Sprott, Ian Nimmo, Archie McArthur and Freddy Anderson, in addition to incisive comments in the course of writing from Mike Paterson.

And for those who helped me on my way, such as my daughters Alison Hill, Jane Livingstone and Lesley Manners in Glasgow, Dunfermline and Newcastle respectively, also good friends like the Logans in Helensburgh, the Patersons in Falkirk, Mike Westcott in Edinburgh, Mr & Mrs Stuart Jeffray in Gifford, Mr & Mrs Iain Crawford in North Berwick, Mr & Mrs Bob Adams in Aberdour, Mr & Mrs Hugh Grant in Inverness, Dick Beach at Dunkeld House Hotel, Grant Sword at the Clifton Hotel, Nairn and Mrs Muriel Thake in Banchory – I give them all thanks for bed and board and encouragement.

Burns made *his* travels in the 17th century by horse, but I was able to retrace his footsteps by horse-power, thanks to Douglas Robertson and the staff of Gauld's of Maryhill, Glasgow who loaned me a car to go *On the Trail of Robert Burns* in Scotland.

I have been involved with Burns and Burns matters now for nearly fifty years but there is not a year goes by in which I don't learn something more about him. I am, therefore, grateful to Gavin MacDougall and Luath Press for giving me this opportunity of discovering yet another trail to Scotland's great literary hero.

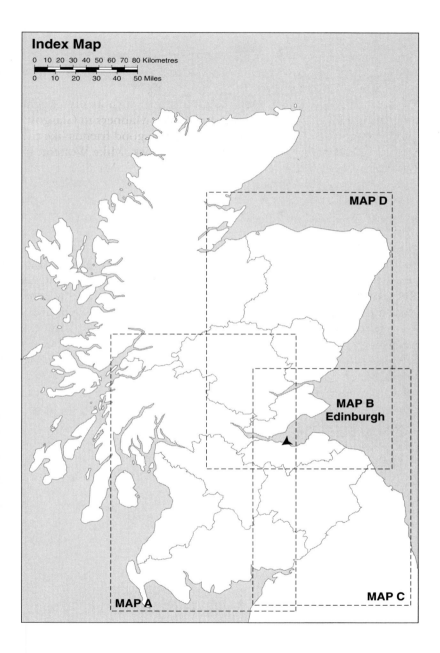

Index Map

0 10 20 30 40 50 60 70 80 Kilometres

0   10   20   30   40   50 Miles

MAP D

MAP B
Edinburgh

MAP A

MAP C

Map A – West of Scotland and West Highlands

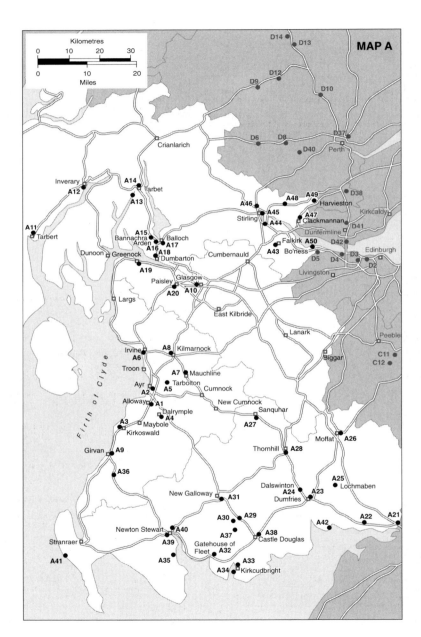

A1 – Alloway pp. xx,1,49,97,148,151
William Burnes builds cottage 1757 and starts market garden. Robert Burns born 25 January 1759. Baptised as Presbyterian by Rev William Dalrymple of Ayr 26 January. William Burnes begins writing his *Manual of Christian Belief*. Robert attends Campbell's school at Alloway Mill 1765. When school closes, John Murdoch hired to teach Burnes children at cottage.

A2 – Ayr pp.xxv,5,7,109,152,153
Robert walks to Ayr for lessons in French and Latin from John Murdoch 1773. Attends School there for a time. Old Ayr Brig the inspiration for *The Brigs o'Ayr* in 1786.

A3 – Kirkoswald pp.9,98
Summer term at Hugh Roger's school 1775. Inspired by Peggy Thomson, the 'charming fillette' next door. Visited on first Galloway Tour 1793. 'Soutar Johnny' Cottage in Main St.

A4 – Dalrymple p.9
Robert and Gilbert attend school week in 1773. Robert attends dancing classes 1775.

A5 – Tarbolton pp.10,21,89,95
Bachelors' Club founded by Burns and others on 11 November 1780 in the upper back-room of an alehouse in the Sandgate. The building is now a museum. Inducted into St David's Lodge No 174 on 4 July 1781.

A6 – Irvine pp.1,12,21,58,142
Sent to learn flax-dressing with the Peacocks in the Glasgow Vennel 1781. Meets Captain Richard Brown, January 1782.

A7 – Mauchline pp.xxi,xxviii,21,53,58,76,79,96,107,145
Meets Jean Armour, one of the Mauchline Belles, during Race Week 1784. Writes *The Jolly Beggars* after night in Poosie Nancie's Inn 1785. Stayed at Johnny Dow's tavern in 1787. Civil marriage to Jean in Gavin Hamilton's office in April 1788. They set up their first house in the village.

A8 – Kilmarnock pp.xxv,17,18,21, 58,109,152,153
612 copies of *Poems, Chiefly in the Scottish Dialect*, published by John Wilson's printing press at the Star Inn Close off King St. on 31 July 1786. Meets William Muir, Tam Samson.

A9 – Girvan
Stayed overnight on way back to Dumfries after first Galloway Tour with Syme 1793.

A10 – Glasgow pp.xxv,57,58
Lodged at the Black Bull Inn in Argyle St. Meets Dr George Grierson. Got an order for 50 books from John Smith, the bookseller. Met up with Captain Richard Brown from Irvine – 'had one of the happiest occasions of my life' at the Black Bull. Also stayed at the Saracen's Head Tavern in the Gallowgate in subsequent visits until 1791. Bought dress material for Jean's wedding dress from Robert McIndoe, the draper, in Virginia St. in 1788 at a cost of four pounds, six shillings and ninepence! Betty Burns, his daughter by Anna Park married a Glasgow soldier, Private John Thomson, and lived in Pollokshaws in 1814. She is buried there. 40,000 Glaswegians paid a shilling each to the *Glasgow Citizen* newspaper to put up a statue to Burns. Most of them crowded into George Square on 25 January 1877 to see it unveiled. The Burns Room in the Mitchell Library in Anderston has one of the finest Burns collections in the world, and in 1999, the City of Glasgow bought the original manuscript of Auld Lang Syne for almost 120,000 pounds to add to it.

A11 – Tarbert p.59
The unlikely starting place for his West Highland your in 1787.

A12 – Inveraray pp.59,60,66
An unhappy visit to the Duke of Argyll who was busy.

A13 – Arrochar pp.57,59
Wrote to Ainslie about 'savage streams, savage mountains and savage inhabitants'.

A14 – Tarbert
Stayed at inn. Wrote a poem on the innkeeper's daughter.

A15 – Bannachra
'Fell in with a merry party at a Highland gentleman's hospitable mansion [Cameron House]... Danced till the ladies left us...'

A16 – Arden
Met Tobias George Smollett, of the famous author's family.

A17 – Balloch p.61
Thrown from his horse in a race with a 'breekless' Highlander.

A18 – Dumbarton pp.52,60,61
Given Freedom of the Burgh.

A19 – Greenock pp.20,57
Supposed visit to see Mary Campbell's grave and visit Campbell family in the hope of retrieving the Bible given to Highland Mary but was rebuffed by her family.

A20 – Paisley pp.17,28,54,61,89
Meets Alexander Pattison and Dr John Taylor. Visits Taylor family.

A21 – Sark p.49
Point near Gretna at which Burns crossed the border and returned into Scotland 2 June 1787.

A22 – Annan pp.49,52
'Overtaken on the way by an old fish of a shoemaker...'.

A23 – Dumfries pp.xxi,xxv,50,52, 80,96,101,109,152,153
Given freedom of the burgh on June 4. Burns moved to Wee Vennel (now Bank St) in Nov 1791. 19 May 1793, moves to Mill Brae (now Burn St). Joins Royal Dumfries Volunteers 1795. Mausoleum at St Michael's Kirkyard built by public subscription in 1819 to a design by T.F. Hunt, restored in 1936 by Herman Cowthraa. The Globe Inn, established c1610, was Burns's local, ('for these many years my favourite howff) and still operates as a tavern.

A24 – Dalswinton pp.50, 52,75
Home of Patrick Miller, Burns's landlord while at Ellisland.

A25 – Lochmaben pp.52,144
Given freedom in 1787 (unauthenticated despite Burns's letter of 9 Dec 1789). Burns visits Maria Riddell here while at Brow in 1796.

A26 – Moffat pp.xxi,52,134
Jean Lorimer of the 'lint-white locks' lived at Craigieburn. Burns wrote many songs on her as Chloris. James Clarke, the schoolmaster was a friend.

A27 – Sanquhar pp.52,91,96
Posted *Ae Fond Kiss* to 'Clarinda' 27 Dec 1791.

A28 – Thornhill p.53
Passed through on 1787 tour.

A29 – Parton p.122
Passed through on 1793 tour with John Syme.

A30 – Airds p.122
Passed through on 1793 tour.

A31 – Kenmure p.122
Stays at Kenmure Castle with Mr and Mrs John Gordon. Writes ode on dog.

A32 – Gatehouse of Fleet p.132
Ruins good riding boots in 1793. Gets drunk with Syme at the Murray Arms Hotel in 1793. Passes through again Jun 1795.

A33 – Kirkudbright p.52
Meets Lord Selkirk who takes Burns's riding boots for mending by coach to Dumfries. Meets Pietro Urbani.

A34 – St Mary's Isle p.122
Composes 'Selkirk Grace' Extempor.

A35 – Wigtown
Passed through on return from first Galloway tour 1793.

A36 – Daljarrock
Ditto

A37 – Lauriston
Ditto

A38 – Castle Douglas p.133
All alone in the Cullnwark Inn, he drinks port and writes letters by candlelight.

A39 – Newton Stewart
Passed through on second Galloway tour Jun 1795.

A40 – Kroughtree p.133
Visits Patrick Heron and his brother, Major Basil Heron.

A41 – Portpatrick p.134
Visits John Gillespie on behalf of Jean Lorimer.

A42 – Brow pp.xxv,142,144
Takes the waters from Brow Well and immerses himself in the Solway Firth during the first 3 weeks of July 1796. Is visited by John Syme.

A43 – Falkirk p.65
Stayed at Cross Keys Inn. 1889 bust of poet now displayed above newsagent's shop. Visited Carron Iron Works with Nicol. Refused entrance because it was a Sunday.

A44 – Bannockburn pp.65,124
In the Gaelic – 'the stream of the white knoll' and the field of Bruce's victory over King Edward II's English army on 24 June 1314. Burns saw the hole, or borestone, where Bruce set up his standard and 'said a prayer for old Caledonia'.

A45 – Stirling pp.xxv,66,76
Stayed at James Wingate's Inn (third floor, north-east corner), now the Golden Lion Hotel, King St. Visited Ancient 30 Lodge. Used Glencairn's stylus to cut verse on window pane.

A46 – Dunblane
Smallest cathedral city in Scotland by the banks of Allan Water.

A47 – Clackmannan p.77
'Knighted' by Mrs Bruce of Clackmannan, a descendant of Robert the Bruce. Her after dinner toast was 'Awa Uncos!' (Away strangers!) – so they left.

A48 – Alva p.78
'Storm-steaded at the foot of the Ochel Hills, with Mr Tait of Harvieston and Mr Johnson of Alva.' Wrote to Mr Cruickshank then dined at Alva House but stayed, according to local tradition, at Courthill House, which at that time was Hume's Inn. It is also said that he 'drank ale with Elizabeth 'Lucky' Black from Mauchline who kept an ale-house in Alva'.

A49 – Harvieston p.76
Visited Mrs Hamilton and family with Dr Adair for eight days. Sees local sights like Caldron Linn and Rumbling Bridge. Proposed to Margaret Chalmers and refused.

A50 – Bo'ness
'A dirty, ugly place, Borrowstounness... in fine, improven, fertile country...'

Map B – Edinburgh

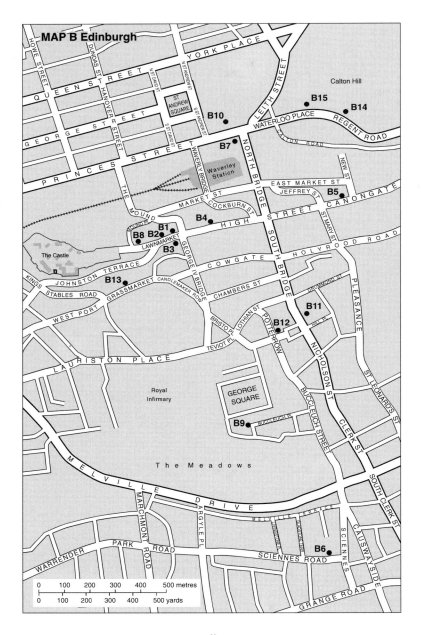

Map C – The Borders

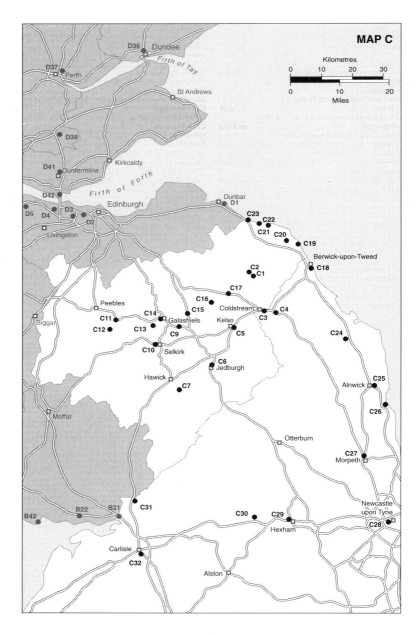

Map D – Highlands and North East

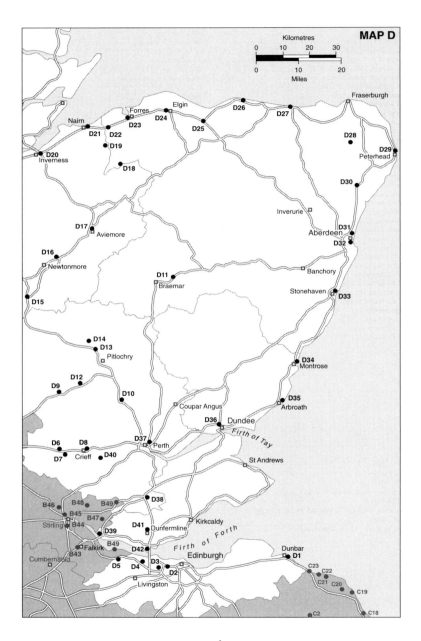

D1 – Dunbar p.42,43
Called on Miss Clark – 'guid enough but no brent new'.

D2 – Corstorphine p.65
Formerly the Cross of Torphine with 15th-century church.

D3 – Kirkliston p.65
Norman church containing Lady Stair's vault.

D4 – Winsburg
Now called Winchburgh.

D5 – Linlithgow pp.52,61,65,76
'What a poor, pimping business is a Presbyterian place of worship stuck in a place of old Popish grandeur...' Given Freedom of Burgh. (Unauthenticated – See Burns Chronicle 1944, p37).

D6 – Comrie
Passes through on Highland tour with Nicol.

D7 – Arbruchill p.66
'A cold reception ...'.

D8 – Crieff p.66
'Sup at Crieff'.

D9 – Kenmore
'Landlord and landlady remarkable characters.' Wrote lines on chimney-piece. Meets Hon Charles Townsend at Taymouth.

D10 – Dunkeld p.66
Sees Druid's Temple – three circles of stones. 'Say prayers in it'.

D11 – Inver
'Sup with Dr Stewart'.

D12 – Aberfeldy p.66
Meets Neil Gow – 'visit his house'. Talk all day about Scottish songs. Dragged away by Nicol.

D13 – Killiecrankie
(Called 'Gilliecrankie'). Sees 'gallant Lord Dundee's stone'.

D14 – Blair Atholl p.67
'Sup with the Duchess – confirmed in my good opinion of my friend, Walker [Josiah]... visit the scenes around Blair in company with Sir William Murray of Ochtertyre... pause at Falls of Bruar'.

D15 – Dalwhinnie
'Snow on the hills 17 feet deep.' Writes A Highland Welcome.

D16 – Pitmain
Now Kingussie, Burns called it 'Pitnim'. Sees Ruthven Castle.

D17 – Aviemore p.68
'A wild romantic spot.' Meets Sir James Grant of Grant.

D18 – Dulsie p.68
'Come through mist and darkness to lie'.

D19 – Kilravock p.69
'Down by the Finhorn to Cawdor... saw the bed in which King Duncan was stabbed. Dined with Mrs Elizabeth Rose'.

D20 – Inverness pp.69,152
Stayed at Ettles Hotel. Dined at Kingsmills House. 'Come over Culloden Muir. Reflections on the field of battle'.

D21 – Nairn p.69
'Fall in with a pleasant enough gentleman, Dr Stewart.'

D22 – Brodie p.69
'To Brodie House to lie – Mr Brodie, truly polite...'.

D23 – Forres p.69
Sees muir where Shakespeare lays witches' meeting.

D24 – Elgin p.69
Sees 'venerable ruins of Elgin Abbey'.

D25 – Fochabers p.69
Dined with Duke and Duchess of Gordon – 'the Duke makes me happier than ever great man did... the Duchess charming, witty and sensible' – but Nicol spoils the party.

D26 – Cullen p.70
'Come to Cullen to lie'.

D27 – Banff p.71
Sees Duff House. Meets Dr Chapman and George Imlach.

D28 – Old Deer
'Come thro' Buchan to Old Dear to lie'.

D29 – Peterhead
'Come along the shore by the famous Bullers of Buchan...'

D30 – Ellon
Passed Ellon House, seat of George Gordon, Earl of Aberdeen – 'entrance denied everybody owing to the jealousy of three score over a kept wench.' [The old Earl had a young English mistress.]

D31 – Old Aberdeen
Passed through.

D32 – Aberdeen pp.xxv,72,152
'A lazy town.' Stayed at New Inn on Castle St. Meets Professor Gordon and Bishop John Skinner, son of the composer of Tullochgorum – 'the best Scotch Song that Scotland ever saw'.

D33 – Stonehaven p.73
A family reunion with the Burnes family. Lie at Laurencekirk.

D34 – Montrose pp.xxv,73
Visited cousin James Burnes, a 'writer' (solicitor) in the town.

D35 – Arbroath p.74
Landed here after sailing along 'wild, rocky coast' in a fishing boat. Met Nicol who preferred to go on by coach.

D36 – Dundee p.74
'Low-lying but pleasant town.' Sees Broughty Castle.

D37 – Perth pp.xxv,74
Visits 'Scoon' (Scone Palace) and Castle Gowrie.

D38 – Kinross p.74
'Come to Kinross to lie... a fit of the colic...'.

D39 – Ochtertyre p.78
One of the two Ochtertyres. This one, in Kincardine near Stirling, was home of Sir John Ramsay who tried to turn Burns towards drama.

D40 – Ochtertyre p.75
This other Ochtertyre in Strathearn near Crief. At the first was John Ramsay and at the second, Sir William Murray, a cousin of Graham of Fintry. Burns visited both, and while with Sir William met Euphemia Murray for whom he wrote a song – Blythe Was She.

D41 – Dunfermline p.77
Visited ruined Abbey and Church. Burns went into the pulpit while Adair mounted the cutty stool. Burns recreated the harangue he received from Rev Daddy Auld at Mauchline when Burns was one of seven receiving the rebuke that Sunday.

D42 – North Queensferry p.74
Another tradition was that John Morrison rowed Burns and Adair across the Forth to Leith, but there is no substantiation of this. What is true is that his formal tours finished here at Queensferry.

Preface

You have doubtless, Sir, heard my story, heard it it with all its exagger-
ations; but as my actions, & my motives for action, are peculiarly like
myself, & that is peculiarly like nobody else, I shall just beg a leisure-
moment & a spare-tear of you, until I tell my own story my own way...

In this letter to John Arnot, written in 1785, the year before his
jump to fame, Burns is as honest with himself as he is with his cor-
respondent, and I can think of no better way to open this book on
his journeys. He goes on –

I have been all my life, Sir, one of the rueful-looking, long-visaged sons
of Disappointment – A damned Star has always kept my zenith, & shed
its baleful influence, in that emphatic curse of the prophet – 'And
behold, whatsoever he doeth, it shall not prosper!' I rarely hit where I
aim; & if I want anything, I am almost sure never to find it where I seek
it. For instance, if my pen-knife is needed, I pull out twenty things – a
plough-wedge, a horse-nail, an old letter or a tattered rhyme, in short,
every thing but my pen-knife; & that at last, after a painful, fruitless
search, will be found in the unsuspected corner of an unsuspected
pocket, as if on purpose thrust out of the way...

The letter continues in the same vein, but it is enough to let us
see a disarming, self-deprecating, charming young man as human
as the rest of us but who had that certain something even then that
lifts some of us 'abune the lave'. No doubt he signed his letter,
Robert Burnes, the name he was born with but not the name the
world knows. Yet it was as such that he knew himself then, at the
start of his public life – Robert Burnes.

The name is said to derive from a stream called the Burnhouse
in Argyll where Walter Campbell, an ancestor of the family, was
born. He is said to have changed his name from Campbell to
Burnhouse in a period of political disaffection when he took his
family to safety in the North-East of Scotland. In time the surname
was corrupted to Burness, and then to Burnes, and finally to Burns
by the poet himself in 1786.

Robert Burns was born at Alloway (A1) in Ayrshire, Scotland, on 25 January 1759, the first son of William Burnes (1721-84), a market-gardener from the Mearns in the North-East of Scotland, and Agnes Broun or Brown (1732-1820), who came from Craigenton, Maybole, in the coastal South-West. The infant was christened next day in the Presbyterian religion of his father by the Reverend William Dalrymple of Ayr and named after his grandfather, Robert Burnes, a tenant-farmer from Clochnahill, near Dunotter in Kincardineshire, who had married Isobel Keith of Criggie in Dunotter. This Robert Burnes was the son of James Burnes (1656-1743) who was the son of Walter Burness (d.1670), the tenant of 'sixty acres of Scotch measure' at Brawlinmoor in the parish of Glenbervie.

On his mother's side, the Browns were a widespread and popular family in Ayrshire and their name had a Norman root, de Brun. Agnes Broun, daughter of Gilbert Broun, a tenant-farmer, had already been betrothed to a ploughman, William Nelson, when she met William Burnes at the Maybole Fair in 1756. She preferred the second William and they were married on 15 December in the following year.

It must be remembered that for much of his boyhood, his father and his brother were the only companions the boy Burns had. This explains much of the later Burns – the gravity that underlay the gaiety, the fits of melancholy that fell about him like a shroud from time to time, the seriousness of his social stand. All these things were part of the paternal legacy and the influence of a remarkable father on an extraordinary son. Similarly, Burns's recklessness, some would say fecklessness and apparent instability of character, were more often than not a deliberate challenge to the conventions of his time and erupting symptoms of the frustration he must have felt at having been born to a station that denied him the opportunities to realise his talents to the full. That he did what he did in the time he was given was astonishing enough, and we should be grateful for it.

We shall see that Burns needed to *be* in love almost as much as he needed to write poems and songs *about* love. There were more than three hundred songs in his output, more than half of which were about women. A great misconception, if that is the right word, about Burns is his sex-drive. My dear old mother – God rest her – who was a highly intelligent but not widely-read (if one exempts Catherine Cookson) Glasgow housewife of Irish stock, could not stand Rabbie Burns, as she called him. 'A right dirty auld man' was her summing up of the poet. She had only heard all the half-truths about him and I doubt if she ever read a word he wrote. This was not her fault. She had never been encouraged to read Burns, even though my father – God rest him too – was what was called a 'Burns man'. You see, not so long ago, Burns was thought to be the preserve of men only, and Protestant men at that, and further, Masonic Protestant men. He was denied to so many Scots and yet he is considered Scotland's national poet.

My mother's 'dirty auld man' never got to be old and he certainly wasn't 'dirty' in his relationships with, or attitudes to, the women in his life. There was nothing furtive or salacious or mean in any of his actions, and even when he was cruel to his future wife in a rare act of brutish assault, he told the world all about it in a letter to a friend – who told the world!

The man who was Burns never lost an element of boyishness in his relations with women. The Tarbolton bachelor was an innocent, and even the Edinburgh roué was as much a victim as any of his supposed conquests. Like any poet, he protested rather too much where women were concerned and very often they were no more than a pretext for a lyric. Women would never had liked him as much as they did had he not liked them. He honoured women and their sex, and he proved it by publicly trumpeting his every liaison in charming lines which have become as much part of Scotland's literary heritage as they are of his own posterity. Burns marked his loves by enshrining them in matchless songs, and by so doing, he made his heroines as immortal as himself.

In this context, much has been made – too much perhaps – of his illegitimate children. There were five at most – one in Mauchline (A7), two in Edinburgh, one in Dumfries (A23) and perhaps one in Moffat (A26); and this in an age when any gentleman could have as many children as he liked outside marriage as long as he paid the required amount to buy the mother off or took in the child. Burns did both in the instances where he was involved except in the case of the two Edinburgh serving girls who dealt with him via a writ – *in meditatione fugae* – although never in any sense was he 'running away'. He had gone back to Jean Armour as he always knew he would. He never considered the two sets of twins he had by Jean before their marriage as anything other than legal off-spring. Within the eight years of their marriage they had another five children, and of the total of nine only three boys survived into old and very respectable age.

In all this discussion of Burns and his sex life, there are two facts that should not be ignored. The first is that Burns did not transgress until his father was dead, and when he did (with Bess Paton, a serving-girl at Mossgiel), he celebrated the event in 1785 by writing the first ever lines addressed to the result of that love act – the bastard wean. It says as much for his sense of fitness and proportion as for his new pride in fatherhood. He took care of the little Elizabeth for the rest of her life, and it is not a little ironic that a recent peer of the realm (Lord Weir) took equal pride in claiming descent from this Burns by-blow. Burns was his own best answer to his critics, as in his *Address to the Unco Guid*:

> *Before ye gie poor Frailty names,*
> *Suppose a change o' places?*
> *A weel-loved lad, convenience snug,*
> *A treacherous inclination,*
> *Well, let me whisper in your lug,*
> *You're aiblins nae temptation!*
> *Then gently scan your brother man,*
> *Still gentler sister woman.*
> *Tho' they may gang a-kennin wrang,*
> *To step aside is human.*
> *One point must still be greatly dark,*
> *The moving why they do it?*
> *And just as lamely can ye mark*
> *How far perhaps they rue it.*
> *Who made the heart, 'tis He alone*
> *Decidedly can try us.*
> *He knows each chord its various tone*

Each spring its various bias,
Then at the balance, let's be mute,
We never can adjust it.
What's done we partly may compute,
We know not what's resisted...

Burns knew only too well what was resisted – even though my mother would never believe it. Dr Bill Murray makes a very good point in his study of the poet as liberationist. He is of the opinion that Burns speaks best for women when he speaks *as* a woman in his lyrics. Burns represents their feelings in the situation described and never better, as Dr Murray declares, than in that hymn to the married state, *John Anderson, my jo*, which many, like the good doctor, consider the greatest of all his love-songs. Burns believed in marriage and every line of the song shows it.

John Anderson, my jo, John,
When we were first acquent,
Your locks were like the raven,
Your bony brow was brent;
But now your brow is beld, John,
Your locks are like the snaw;
But blessings on your frosty pow,
John Anderson, my Jo.
John Anderson, my jo, John,
We clamb the hill the gither,
And monie a cantie day, John,
We've had wi' ane anither;
Now we maun totter down, John,
And hand in hand we'll go;
And sleep thegither at the foot,
John Anderson, my Jo.

If Robert Burns had been born to the roll of a thunderstorm then it might be said his brief life was lit by flashes of lightning. The first occurred when he discovered books, the next when he discovered women, and the third – and most important – was when he discovered that he could write. This was the spark that lit the flame that set alight all he would ever want to do in his life. From the time he wore 'the only tied hair in the parish' and wrapped his *fillemot* plaid about his shoulders in his distinctive way, he was rehearsing for his role as a player on a larger stage than that offered by Mauchline belles and Tarbolton bachelors. Every spoken word so carefully considered, every written line even more carefully contrived in his youthful excesses away from the grinding farm, was a bullet in the armoury he devised to bring down the walls of prejudice and custom that kept him and his fellow-peasants immured in their humble station.

Given his imaginative calibre, there was little need for him to travel even to the extent that he did in his five Scottish tours. He could have roamed quite easily through the continent of his own mind and found stimulation enough there, but it did him no harm to move out of his circle even if he was not always easily accepted in the other circles that widened out to him. That he was confident enough to move out at all says something for him. In his class there were people who lived out long lives without moving a mile from where they were born. They saw no need, and followed the pattern of their simple lives just as their ancestors had done. In a way, this is an enviable acceptance of fate, but Burns knew early that a static, earth-rivetting existence was not for him. He was curious about the world and about men and their ways, and he set himself to find out about them. There was also something – some devil – driving him on. Basically, it might only have been a profound discontent. He thought his talents deserved better than a cotter's lot. And he was right.

His every hand-written scrap was a step on the way, first to local fame as a rhymer, then contemporary national acclaim as a bard, and finally to an international renown which even today shows little prospect of diminishing. His public life spanned no more than a decade, and the travels which will concern us now hardly took him further than a few days' riding from his birthplace, yet Robert Burns must be seriously considered today as one of the best-known sons of Scotland.

It all began with a book of rhymes – *Poems, Chiefly in the Scottish Dialect* – a slim volume in blue covers paid for by subscription and published at Kilmarnock (A8) on 31 July 1786. Everything in Burns's life pointed towards this moment and obtained from it. This was the crux, the kernal, the turning point, and on it everything else turned. It was really to sell this book, or collect money due for it, that he undertook his first tour. He maintained that his first Border tour was a holiday, but if it were, it was a working holiday. Similarly, he went off to the North-East on a song search as much as for any other reason, and from Dumfries (A23) he escaped to Galloway more for a bit of peace. The final trip to Brow (A42) can only be described as a desperate measure.

Burns's Scotland is a rough quadrilateral emanating from Dumfries in the South-West, north via Ayr (A2) to Glasgow (A10) and on to Aberdeen (D32) via Stirling (A45) then down again to Edinburgh by way of Montrose (D34) and Perth (D37), to return across country to Dumfries. If one allows for slight extensions to the West Highlands on one side and to Newcastle (C28) on the other, that is the full extent of Burns's travels in the world. It is not much for an age which included the Grand Tour through Europe as almost mandatory for every young gentleman coming out into his majority. To travel with a friend or one's tutor to Paris, Rome and Athens, and return by way of Spain or Portugal before taking up a full social life in London or Bath, was the done thing in Burns's time, as his fellow countryman, Boswell, did from Auchinleck.

Burns had to set out from Mossgiel sustained by his own certainty. For him Edinburgh would serve happily as an Athens, Glasgow would be his London, Aberdeen his Rome, Inverness could be his Paris, Stirling his Lisbon, Perth his Madrid and Dumfries would stand in rather neatly for Bath. Apart from a marginal excursion into Northern England, his would be a strictly Caledonian odyssey. After all, his interests were totally chauvinistic. He had said himself that he only wanted to see his native land. It was her songs he sang, and for all his bookish knowledge of the world and his unexpected conversational skills, his Muse still spoke with an Ayrshire accent.

The first appeal for subscription in 1786 had made no bones about this. It had openly stated that what was being sold were

'Scotch poems by Robert Burns', and however 'elegantly printed' or 'neatly stitched', the three-shilling package made no concessions to the then current vogue for Englishness among the literati. In this, Burns was performing an underrated service for Scottish literature and the Scots tongue. His work in verse saved some words for all time, just as his work on the songs would preserve the ancient fragments. Altogether, it was no mean feat for one little book. 618 copies were eventually printed and they were all sold in a matter of weeks. Of course, they were pre-sold by the very fact of having been subscribed for, but the instant clamour for a second edition was proof that he had hit the mark, although he diffidently admitted:

For me, an aim I never fash
I rhyme for fun...

Yet he took it seriously enough to ride all over Ayrshire chasing subscribers, and he would do the same all over Scotland east of the Caledonian Canal. It pleased him enormously to be a poet in print, even though he had only done it to make what he called 'Jamaica money', this despite the fact that the original notice also stated that the author had 'not the most distant *mercenary* views in publishing'. There are certain things one must say to sell books and one must accept it as just one of those professional lies. He genuinely relished seeing his verse in a book and a good part of him would have allowed that for nothing, but not all of him. He later refused to sell a song, but he was willing to sell a poem, and to do so, he was ready to travel to the ends of the earth – as long as he didn't have to leave Scotland.

If one is on the trail of Robert Burns in Scotland, one doesn't have to look very far. He stares out from dishtowels, ashtrays, teapots, teaspoons, aprons (non-Masonic) and just about every kind of fabric that can take the Nasmyth reproduction. Burns is a modern Scottish industry and his image is available on anything and everything. This mass imaging is not good for his status as a serious artist in words. He is the Archangel and Patron Saint of Tourism and is canonised forever as a brand. It will be difficult to prise him off all the hoardings. Whether it is as full-size statue, stone bust, paper-weight or postage stamp, in wood, ceramics, cast-iron or plastic, this is the ubiquitous Burns everyone knows, or at least recognises. It is a wonder he is still recognisable. But is this the Burns we're really looking for?

Guy de Maupassant tells us that the traveller takes himself with him wherever he goes. So who did Burns take – the farmer or the poet, the exciseman or the song-maker? Was the 27-year old who set out for Duns (C2) on that first May day really sure himself? He had a finger-hold on fame and that was about all he was certain of – he wanted a good, firm grasp of that elusive cup of success, and he wanted it brimming over, but he was by no means sure of how to get it. He had a realistic idea of his own abilities but no certain plan how to use them. He hoped he might get some kind of indication along the way. He would wait and see what happened. Many of us treat our own life-journey like that – we just keep going and see how it goes. The thing is to keep going. However, in order to do so, we need a goal, a purpose, a vision. What was Burns's? Certainly he wanted to make money out of his books, but if he had really been so mercenary, he would have been cannier with publisher Creech and drawn up a lucrative contract with Thomson to sell his songs. He was not at all a stupid man but he was a lazy man of business, and one must therefore conclude that he did not give himself entirely to the commerce of making his way with words work for him. Burns, the horseman, never broke into the hot sweat of a gallop towards fortune. Poetry, he thought, would be its own reward. Somehow, everything would land in his lap. His talent would ensure that. But even genius needs to be worked at. It needs to be sold, like everything else. As Robert Louis Stevenson remarked, everybody lives by selling something. What Burns sold best was himself, but by the time he caught on, it was too late. He was just getting into his stride when he was forced out of the running.

Robert Burns was hardly into his maturity when he died, and one can only lament the loss to Scotland and to literature of a gray-haired Burns. He did so much, but he might have achieved much more had he been given the years. All the signs showed that he was learning fast and another decade would have seen him at the height of his powers. As it was, Dumfries so frustrated him that perhaps he was glad to get out of the constant struggle in the end – to escape.

The same sense of escape applied to his tours. They were a means of getting on to the open road to feel the free wind on his face. As long as he was on the road he was free himself – free of the demands of Gilbert and his family at Mossgiel, of Jean Armour and *her* family in Mauchline (A7), Creech and his dilatory accounting, and of the insistent need to make up his mind on what he was going to do with his life. As long as he was travelling, he didn't need to decide. The thing was, to keep moving. His only responsibility was to get from here to there, wherever it was, and to make sure there was room at the inn and a bottle on the table. After all, wasn't it supposed to be a holiday too? For the duration of the tours at least, he was Robert Burns – Tourist.

We begin where he began – at Alloway.

CHAPTER I

The Burns Country

(25 January 1759 to 27 November 1786)
Alloway – Ayr – Kirkoswald – Irvine – Mauchline – Kilmarnock

Alloway

There was a lad 'twas born in Kyle
An' whatna day, an' whatna style...

KYLE, NEARLY 400 SQUARE MILES of it, stands bang in the centre of Ayrshire, with its long coastline facing Ailsa Craig which guards those waters where the Irish Sea meets the Atlantic Ocean. The sea-port of Irvine (A6) is to the north, the River Doon to the south and the River Ayr runs through it from east to west. Kyle is one of the three ancient bailiwicks or regalities of the Strathclyde region, the others being Cunninghame to the north and Carrick south. This is the heart of what has come to be called the Burns Country and where our Robert Burns trail has to begin. Here the poet learned to walk and talk and it is here we must look for his first footprints.

The clay and timbered two-roomed thatched cottage where Burns was born on 25 January 1759 still exists and stands conspicuously by the roadside in the trim, prim little village that has grown up around it. The Brig o' Doon, where Tam o'Shanter's mare, Maggie, made her mythical jump, is only a little way to the right of it, and Alloway Kirk, where the witches danced to the Devil's bagpipe in the same poem, a little more to the left as it looks out on the world. Alloway Cottage (A1) is right in the centre of things Burnsian.

Old Brig o' Doon, Alloway

Like the Cottage itself, the village of Alloway has grown a

little smug over the years, quietly proud of its worldwide fame, although you would never get one of today's well-heeled commuter-villagers to admit it. The whole of Alloway has become a much-sought-after property area. Its residents are, for the most part, affluent and respectable, and their high-quality environment attracts the same kind of high-quality, international tourist to the Burns places and outlets, although they rarely visit them themselves. It's not so much a case of familiar contempt than a good intention to get round to it some day – when they're not so frightfully busy.

The Cottage itself, thanks to its constantly revolving turnstile revenue, is almost as rich, and the continued Council care, following on the Burns Federation's devout management for more than a century, has given the building an air of sanctity synonymous with many much-loved historical monuments. This, I suppose, is almost inevitable given the reverence for Burns and everything associated with him, but it is hard to believe that this was once a home rudely lived in by man and beast. Its present artificialised, story-book finish would render it unrecognisable to the man who built it in 1756. William Burnes, the poet's father, made it with his own hands; it was what Burns himself called 'an auld, cley biggin', which fell apart at the first real storm-wind from the Atlantic in 1759 and had to be rebuilt entirely. It must have been well rebuilt for it is still there, echoing to the tread of foreign feet and the click and purr of cameras.

Alloway Burns Cottage

Yet for all its commercial accommodation and sophisticated PR, one must always remember, with a catch of the breath, that it was here, in the little bed, that Robert Burns was born. It was this air he first breathed, and this light he first caught. It's a braking thought among all the illustrations and explanations that surround one.

Our Monarch's hindmost year but ane
Was five-and-twenty days begun,
'Twas then a blast o' Janwar win'
Blew hansel in on Robin...

Burns's younger brother, Gilbert, later explained the matter
more prosaically in a letter to Dr Currie, Burns's first biographer,
in 1803:

When my father built his cley biggin, he put in two stone jambs, as they
are called, and a lintel carrying up the chimney in his clay-gable.
The consequence was, that as the gale subsided, the jambs remaining
firm, threw it off its centre; and, one very stormy morning, when my
brother was only nine or ten days old, a little before daylight, a part of
the gable fell out, and the rest appeared so shattered, that my mother,
with the young poet, had to be carried through the storm to a neighbour's house, where they remained a week, till their own dwelling was
adjusted.

The neighbour mentioned was John Tennant of Glenconner,
'gude auld Glen, the ace and wale of honest men' Burns wrote of
him. He also called him 'a worthy, intelligent farmer, my father's
friend and my own'. He later became factor to the Countess of
Glencairn at Ochiltree and rented the farm of Glenconner. He had
four sons, all known to Burns in later life. James, the oldest, was the
subject of a Verse Epistle from the Bard which included the lines:

Mony a laugh and mony a drink
And aye enough o needfu' clink.

The Tennant family was never to be short of 'clink'. The second son, John, went to school with Burns in Ayr (A2) for a time,
but was never to achieve much. The third, David, became a sailor
('the manly tar') or more exactly, a privateer, and when he retired,
after losing a hand in battle at sea, he refused a knighthood and
became a Freemason. The fourth son, Charles, was a weaver,
('Wabster Charlie' to Burns) and he also refused a knighthood. All
kinds of honours came to his posterity, mainly owing to Charlie's
invention of a bleaching process which made his fortune. He

3

moved to Glasgow where he built a factory at St Rollox (with the highest chimney in Europe at the time), and founded the Tennant empire which included a brewery which still exists today. Charles Tennant, like Burns, maintained his egalitarian views, even though he did this from a large mansion in Blythswood Square. He was a stout champion of the Reform movement in Scotland, and had he not been so well connected, this might have got him into trouble. The same was to apply to Burns in the years to come.

John Murdoch, the 18-year old school master hired by William Burnes to teach his two sons, described the Cottage as – 'with the exception of a little straw, literally a tabernacle of clay'. He also referred to it pedantically as 'the argillaceous fabric' but we must remember that his was an 18th-century mind, and it was this mind which influenced Burns at the age of seven still playing about the door under his mother's eye. Murdoch, the bookish youth with the fine writing hand, made the market-gardener's son a precocious English scholar. Not a Scottish one – Burns was to do that for himself. At the beginning he was to imbibe a totally English influence from his first formal teaching under John Murdoch. Murdoch wrote later:

> In this cottage, of which I myself was at times an inhabitant, I really believe there dwelt a larger portion of content than in any Palace in Europe. 'The Cottar's Saturday Night' will give some idea of the temper and manners that prevailed there.

One has to remember that Murdoch's tastes were defined by his own education which pointed him towards classicism combined with a sentimental regard for the peasantry. This sort of thing would be exactly to his taste, although one feels that in *The Cottar's Saturday Night* Burns was writing less from personal memory than from a desire to paint an ideal picture.

> *With joy unfeign'd, brothers and sisters meet,*
> *And each for other's weelfare kindly spiers:*
> *The social hours, swift-wing'd, unnotic'd fleet;*
> *Each tells the unco that he sees or hears.*
> *The patents partial eye their hopeful years;*

Anticipation forward points the view;
The mother, wi' her needle and her sheers,
Gars auld claes look amaist as weel's the new;
The father mixes a' wi' admonition due.

When William Burnes moved two miles inland to Mt Oliphant farm in 1766, he let the cottage and its cultivated seven acres of market garden to various tenants until 1781 when he sold it outright to the Incorporation of Shoemakers in Ayr (A2). They in turn let it out as an alehouse which it remained until it was 'rescued' by a body called the Alloway Monument Trustees who, like any well-meaning monumental authority, gutted the place and restored it to what it is today – a clean, tidy, over-painted, over-monitored edifice that might even be improved by a whiff of ale and the sound of a good guffaw. Murdoch called it a 'tabernacle' but I'm sure he never meant a sepulchre.

However, it is the newer building, the Museum adjacent to the Cottage, that worries me more. In the plain, stone building there is a priceless collection of Bursiana, but one feels that these books, papers and paintings could be better housed elsewhere than shoulder to shoulder with the Cottage. Burns seems uncomfortable there, weighed down by relics and memorabilia, hemmed in by glass cases and Victorian bric-a-brac. Much of it is tastefully done, but much is not. What is treasurable should be moved to an extended Burns Centre just along the road and the present building knocked down. This may sound draconian, but the Cottage and the Museum are different buildings from different ages and make an incongruous pairing. The presence of a turnstile at the Museum only adds to the daunting schoolhouse feel to the place. It is not Burns. It is a relic of another time and another way of thinking about him.

If the whole Museum site were restored to a garden, the Cottage would stand out superbly. After all, it was originally called The New Gardens, and the good intention of the Victorian Burnsians had been to return the place to what it was. Let it be a garden again, and Burns's Cottage would become its natural self and smell of flowers instead of municipal floor polish. Think of a

5

Robert Burns garden – every flower a song, every tree a poem, and winding paths and waterways flowing among natural things. But to our Trail... William Burnes was *not* a horticulturist.

My father was a farmer upon the Carrick border
And carefully he bred me in decency and order

By any standards he was a remarkable man, and it was in no small measure due to his strenuous efforts that the boy Burns developed his love of the word, both in the sound it made and the effect it had on the page. William, a Northerner from the Mearns, was a gardener to Provost Fergusson of Ayr on his property at Doonside, and it was this man who gave him a start on his own land at Alloway. William was what might be called a peasant aristocrat. Though his parents are said to have had cutlery on the table, he was not born to privilege, yet he never saw himself as under-privileged. He had a mind and was unafraid to use it. He had made himself as well read as he could and he passed on to his first son his reverence for learning and the power of the printed word. He developed a high moral stance based on the Presbyterian Bible and an unswerving faith in a stern Scotch God. How this pillar of rectitude came to marry Agnes Brown, the red-headed, fun-loving, song-filled daughter of a Maybole farmer, is just one of the mysteries in the story of Burns, but each is imprinted in the two opposing sides of him. We cannot begin to understand Burns until we understand this.

From his mother he got his gypsy good looks, from his father he got his mind. From his mother came the sensual strain, from his father came his life-long sense of guilt about it. His character was a constant see-sawing between these two extremes, the righteous mind in constant war with the animal body. He was, in fact, the synthesis of a unique parentage. He was both Prospero and Puck. He sprang, hugely gifted and fully formed as it were, out of this complete contradiction. His pedigree boasted no literary figure of any size. Nor has it thrown up any in his own descendants since. Burns was a one-off. In short, he was a genius.

On the estate of Doonholm, a mile or so inland from Alloway,

Mt Oliphant was the first farm Burns knew, and at 40 pounds a year the 70 acres were a bad bargain from the start. The soil was poor and unyielding, and the Burnes family (now with six children) knew the roughest of times. As the oldest, Robert had to take the brunt of it. The younger brother, Gilbert, wrote:

> My brother, at the age of thirteen, assisted in threshing of corn, and at fifteen was the principal labourer on the farm... I doubt not, but the hard labour and sorrow of this period of his life, was in great measure, the cause of that depression of spirits with which Robert was so often afflicted throughout his whole life afterwards.

In 1769, Provost Fergusson died. He had been a kind and understanding landlord, well aware of William's qualities, and happy to wait till things got better. His estate factor, however, was not so patient. He hounded the family for full payment of the arrears and years later Burns was still angry – 'My blood yet boils at the recollection of the scoundrel tyrant's insolent, threatening epistles which used to set us all in tears'. In *The Twa Dogs* he was to write of that same, unnamed factor:

> *Poor tenant bodies, scant o' cash,*
> *How they maun thole a factor's snash:*
> *He'll stamp an' threaten, curse an' swear*
> *While they maun stan', wi' aspect humble,*
> *An' hear it a', an fear an' tremble.*

Ayr

Nothing, however, would deflect the good father from taking every opportunity to throw learning at his sons. He never seemed to make the same efforts for his four daughters, other than to encourage them to read. The Burnes's table was one where reading was encouraged at meals. Books were eaten up with great appetite even when there was little else on the table.

In 1773, John Murdoch returned to Ayrshire from London and set up a school in a house in Ayr (A2), and to Ayr Robert was sent, after he had helped to bring in the harvest, to refresh his

English Grammar and make a start on learning French. He never ceased in later life to show off the little French he had managed to pick up. He also started some Latin, but 'only when I was not in love. Consequently, my studies did not go forward.' Ayr was the county town of Ayrshire and as Robert himself admitted – 'my vicinity to Ayr was a great advantage to me', although it was in that same town he first learned of the 'immense distance' that lay between himself and the sons of 'the noblesse and gentry' who were his new classmates. Burns was never to lose the chip on the shoulder he developed about this. Nevertheless, these stolen school weeks in Ayr must have seemed like heaven on earth after the hell of the farm, or, as he called it, 'the unceasing moil of the galley-slave'. However, there were now some compensations. The thing that kept him from his Latin studies was Love, or rather Sex. Girls. Females. At the age of 15, Burns, the underfed, under-clothed and over-read farm labourer, fell in love. Nellie Kilpatrick was just one summer younger, and it was for this 14-year old girl, in her kirtled skirts (lifted above the knees), he wrote his first song in a harvest field.

> *She dresses ay sae clean and neat,*
> *Baith decent and genteel;*
> *And yet, there's something in her gait,*
> *Gars ony dress look weel.*

Not surprisingly, it was a stilted, self-conscious effort, but then he was a stilted, self-conscious boy. But this little piece of juvenilia, preserved forever in all the collections of the Works, has made both Mt Oliphant and Miss Kilpatrick famous. To both we owe the poet. As he said himself – 'I never thought to turn poet till I got heartily in love, then rhyme and song were, in a manner the spontaneous language of my heart.'

Kirkoswald

Having discovered his delight in the company of the fairer sex, he was to look for it at every opportunity for the rest of his short life. Robert Burns was never NOT to be in love. When, in 1775, he was sent to Hugh Rodger's school at Kirkoswald (A3), a smugglers' village by the sea at that time, to learn Mensuration, Surveying and Dialing, etc, his study of line and form was applied more to Peggy Thomson, 'a charming fillette' who lived next door, who drew from him another song, *Composed in August*:

> *Not vernal show'r to budding flow'rs,*
> *Not Autumn to the Farmer,*
> *So dear can be, as thou to me.*
> *My fair, my lovely Charmer!*

Ten years later, in 1786, he was to give her a Kilmarnock edition of his Poems with the inscription 'once fondly lov'd and still remembered dear'. She had so affected him that he had returned home, in his own words, 'considerably improved' but certainly not in Mensuration, Surveying or Dialing.

From this time on, however, hardly a day was to pass that he did not have a goosefeather in his hand or a song on his lips. And, incredibly, the first notes were heard at Mt Oliphant. The soil may not have yielded William Burnes a living for his growing family, but metaphorical seeds sown here by his oldest son were to take firm root and flower astonishingly. Nothing in Burns's early life had prepared him for poesy and song and yet he came to both like a natural. Against all the odds, he found he could work with words. And he did so, easily and naturally, as if this was what he was born to do.

Dalrymple

Burns first went to this village (A4) by the River Doon when he was about 14. He attended the little school there for a time, but he was to know it better when he went to the dancing school just a few years later. Burns loved dancing and became very good at it. He no doubt also enjoyed the proximity it gave to the girls. He first went to dancing classes in the winter of 1775, 'to give his manners a brush', and was to continue attending each winter until 1779. Yet, he insists, 'no solitaire was less acquainted with the ways of the world', so it was strictly in the interests of self-improvement that he defied his revered father by going. Fortunately for their relationship at least, his father had other, more pressing, matters on his mind.

Tarbolton

At last, in 1777, William Burnes won free of the cruel lease that had tied him so bitterly to a bad farm, and scraping what was left in the barrel, he entered into what seemed a better arrangement at Lochlie (now Lochlea), a much larger farm in the parish of Tarbolton (A5), about ten miles to the north. It would transpire, however, that he had merely exchanged the 70 barren acres of Mt Oliphant for 130 acres of swampland. Lochlie had what farmers call a 'wet bottom'. If it was for his father mainly a transfer of bad luck, for his first son it was the beginning of his greatness, for it was at Lochlie Farm that Robert Burns taught himself to write.

Dr James Mackay, in his seminal Burns biography (Mainstream, Edinburgh 1992), calls this period at Lochlie 'the contented years', and so they might have been, in the light of the poet's volatile life. Even if only for the fact that he had food in his belly and dry clothes on his back, it was an improvement on anything he had known so far. For the first four years at least, in Burns's own phrase – 'we lived comfortably' – and he was able to invest in that inestimable luxury for the working lad – leisure. Time was his for his own purposes and he lost no time in filling the welcome hours.

The Bachelors' Club at Tarbolton was formed primarily for him to practice talking. He and Gilbert, with several other local youths, founded the debating club for the amusement and interest of those young men in the parish who were – 'a professed lover of one or more of the female sex'. One can detect the Burnsian influence. Their meeting-place (now a museum) was a back room on the upper floor of an alehouse in the Sandgate, but the whole thing was really just a platform for Master Robert Burns, a further exercise in self-improvement. He was getting himself ready, for what he wasn't quite sure, but he knew he would need to talk and write in English – to the highest standards.

The Bachelors' Club, Tarbolton

Everything he did in the rehearsal years of his youth had a double purpose – immediate pleasure, of course, but also a reforming or improving aspect. This was in everything he did. Debating took its place with dancing and rhyming not only as his work relief, but as a means towards an end. 'I saw that my father's situation entailed on me perpetual labour', he had said. He was continually looking for a way out – a doorway to fortune – and he knew that, as far as he was concerned, words were the key. He used them in every way possible – in conversations at home with his father who admired his son's gift for what was then termed disputation; in letters written for love-sick friends; in his poetry and re-working of old song-lyrics and in the debates he organised for the Bachelors' Club. He was the accepted leader in his own circle, small as it was, but with each year he was widening it gradually. So far, his horizons were bounded entirely by the parish of Tarbolton, but already he was trying to push beyond this rustic pale.

In his own capacity as a lover of the female sex, he made the first of several serious and determined assaults in that area, but was firmly repulsed by the young lady concerned. It was not the first time that Robert Burns was to be turned down as a marriage suitor, but it left him, as he said – 'in peculiar circumstances of mortification'. What these were he doesn't explain, nor are we completely sure who the girl was. Dr Mackay insists that her name was Elizabeth Gebbie (the heroine of *Fair Eliza*), although other sources have referred to her as Alison or Ellison Begbie. In this respect, what becomes more and more remarkable is the number of ladies who have appeared since Burns's death to claim that they inspired his love songs or had turned him down as a husband. However, Miss Gebbie or Begbie deserves to be remembered if only for the fact that she did inspire, albeit inadvertently, one of his earliest and greatest love songs. Generally, it was his habit to incorporate his heroine's name in the lyric, but not even his nascent genius could have coped with the rhyme required for a name like Begbie! Or even Gebbie! So, for song purposes, she became 'Mary Morrison' and as such she remains immortal. As long as this lovely song is sung, she will be remembered. It was to be the same for so many of his heroines.

> *Tho' this was fair, an' that was braw*
> *And thon the toast o' a' the toon,*
> *I sigh'd, and said amang them a',*
> *'Ye are na Mary Morrison.'*

Hugh MacDiarmid, a modern Bard, and perhaps Scotland's greatest poet after Burns, said he would have given all he had written to have composed that last line – *'Ye are na Mary Morrison'*. Its limpid directness has the secret of all art in it. But, as artists have found in every age, talent does not always pay the rent. Poetry was 'still the darling walk' of his mind, but the 22-year old Burns had a sterner road to walk in the continued battle that survival was to his father. This time, the road led to Irvine.

Irvine

This bustling little town (A6) was once the seaport for the city of Glasgow, but in 1781, when Burns first went there, it was a place of spinners and weavers as well. Flax was a profitable crop and land at Lochlie was put to its cultivation, but heckling, or combing out the fibre, it for the spinners was costly, and Burns (or his father) had the idea that they should do it themselves. So Robert was dispatched to Irvine, with the Bible and Smollet's *Tristram Shandy* in his pocket, to learn something of the heckling trade. It wasn't pleasant work in the dry dust and smells of the Smiddy Bar where the workshop was, and it affected his health almost at once. He fell ill, so seriously that his father had to come to see him through a crisis. Luckily, a Hogmanay revel set fire to the heckling shop, and this put paid to the enterprise and to the investment. Burns returned home 'like a true poet, not worth a sixpence'.

> *O, why the duece should I repine*
> *And be an ill-foreboder?*
> *I'm twenty-three an' five feet nine,*
> *I'll go an be a sodger!*

He didn't, of course, because he had met a sailor called Richard Brown in Irvine and, while on a walk in the Leglen Woods, it was this man who first gave Burns the idea of putting his rhymes and songs into a book. The Irvine project was worthwhile just for this idea alone, because without Brown's suggestion, we might never have known about Burns at all, never mind recognised him now as a world-class poet and song-writer. Captain Richard Brown is an important character in the Robert Burns Story, for during that afternoon in Irvine, he put the germ of an idea into the young man's head:

> *That I, for poor old Scotland's sake,*
> *Some usefu' plan, or book, could make...*

The winter of 1782 saw his second spell at Lochlie, and the lyric spark he had been so assiduously fanning finally caught alight with lively, surging songs like his reworking of another ancient song into his own *Corn Rigs*:

> *The time flew by, wi' tentless heed.*
> *Till 'tween the late and early;*
> *Wi' sma' persuasion she agreed*
> *To see me thro' the barley.*

There was nothing ever forced or artificial about Burns's way with song lyrics. They appeared so easy and effortless, but their charm often hid the work that went into them, although it was pleasurable work for him. This was what he was best at and he knew it. There were distractions, however. Dr Mackay's word for this phase is 'litigious' and it is easy to see why. William Burnes, through a complication of misunderstandings, best intentions and lack of specific terms, particularly with regard to improvements on the farmstead, fell foul of his landlord, David McLure. To William's mind, McLure had not kept his word, and that was sacred to the senior Burnes. On a point of moral principle, he would not yield to the landlord's repeated demands, even when he was taken to court and had his proud name called by the Tarbolton town crier and drummed through the district as a bad debt. His property was put under the threat of sequestration, but still he would not concede his case. The main trouble was that there was nothing in writing. It is something of an irony that, at this time, nothing should be *in writing*, yet at the same time, under the same threatened roof, his own son was building up a body of writing that would have brought in enough money to have settled all his father's debts had he been able to wait long enough. Burns had begun on his first Commonplace Book –

> Observations, Hints, Songs, Scraps of Poetry, etc by Robert Burnes – a man who has little art in making money, still less of keeping it; a man, however, of some sense, a great deal of honesty, and unbounded good will to every creature.

His own words were always to be the best writing about himself.

When he was writing *The Death and Dying Words of Poor Mailie* there was little he could do little to prevent the approaching death of his own good father, whose dying words were an expressed fear for his favourite – 'There's only one of you I fear for'. Yet years before he had said to his wife, 'Wha lives will know that boy'. Now he was dying before he himself could see the fame that was to come to 'that boy'. William's own triumph was that his appeal to the High Court in Edinburgh over his case with McLure was upheld, and he was totally exonerated as he knew he would be. The misfortune was that he received the news on his deathbed.

With his father's death, Burns could now be his own man. He was free. For 25 years the father was a needed restraint on his tempestuous son, but now that rein was off

> *O, leave novels, ye Mauchline belles –*
> *Ye're safer at your spinning-wheel!*
> *Such witching books are baited hooks*
> *For rakish rooks like Rob Mossgiel.*
> *Robert Burns came into his own as Rob Mossgiel.*

When they saw their father's end coming, the Burns brothers had made a plan with the help of Mauchline lawyer, Gavin Hamilton, to leave Lochlie and move over the hill to another farm at Mossgiel just outside Mauchline (A7). Burns entered into the new regime with, as he said, 'a firm resolution' – 'Come, go to, I will be wise!' But in the first two years two harvests were lost, the first due to bad seed, the second a late spring. This upset all his 'new wisdom' and he returned to his old ways 'like a dog to its vomit, or a sow that has been washed to its wallowing in the mire'. However, there is a question of what his 'old ways' were. He hadn't really done anything yet except give himself over to the writing of verse. Gilbert took over the running of the farm and Burns took up his pen to write most of the work by which he was to be known. And it all happened between 1784 and 1786.

In these two short years the words flowed from him like a flood and some of the great pieces were born. 1785 was his *annus mirabilis*. The goose-feather took wings and flew, resulting in such masterpieces as *Holy Willie's Prayer, Death and Doctor Hornbook, To a Mouse, The Jolly Beggars, The Cotter's Saturday Night*, not to mention the songs, verse epistles, epigrams and epitaphs that came to hand as easily as they came to mind. It also signalled another change. In May 1785 he and Gilbert had changed their surname to distance themselves from their father's debts – or perhaps to accommodate the last lines of Robert's *Epistle to William Simpson*:

The Burns Monument,
Mauchline

While Terra Firma on her axis
Diurnal turns,
Count on a friend, in faith and practice,
Robert Burns.

Henceforth, he would use this name. It was almost as if it signalled a centring of his intentions, as if he'd found a clear focus at last.

Also born, however, on 22 May of that same golden year, was his first child, a daughter born out of wedlock to Bess Paton, a live-in serving girl in his father's house. Burns never began any physical relationship with a girl while his father lived, but when that influence was gone...

In Mauchline there dwells six proper young belles,
The pride of the place and its neighbourhood a',
Their carriage and dress, a stranger would guess,
In London or Paris, they'd gotten it a'.
Miss Millar is fine, Miss Markland's divine,
Miss Smith she has wit, and Miss Betty is braw,
There's beauty and fortune to get with Miss Morton;
But Armour's the jewel for me o' them a'.

Jean Armour, the favourite daughter of the Mauchline stonemason, was to become Burns's wife and the constant in his intermittent love life. Theirs was to be a stormy courtship, but in the end she won him as her husband and the loving father of the nine children born to them. Jean knew she had tied herself to a will o' the wisp, but she was the only one who could restrain him because she was the only one who understood him. The other loves would come and go in the verse of a poem or the lilt of a song or in a one-night bed or byre, but she would remain until his death, an anchor and a haven. All she was ever to say of his *affaires* was – 'Our Robin should hae had twa wives'.

A new seriousness overtook him. He was no longer the gadfly romancer with the saffron plaid and the only tied hair in the parish. The death of his father, his own fatherhood, the commitment to Jean, the new-found confidence in his writing, all these things contributed to a new weight in his work. The burst of creativity at Mossgiel was remarkable by any standards, an extraordinary time. Unfortunately, at the same time, there were the first of the many complications in his relationship with Jean. She was pregnant.

Despite Burns's vehement wish to marry her, she was packed off to Paisley (A20) by her irate father to marry a weaver, Andrew Wilson. Burns retaliated by taking up with Mary (or Margaret) Campbell, a local nursery-maid, and planning to emigrate with her to the West Indies. He even booked a nine-guinea passage with a shipping agent in Irvine 'to waft me to the torrid zone'. (Notice the 'me', not 'us' as it would have been if Miss Campbell had been included.) Meantime, Jean had returned to Mauchline. It seemed that the weaver would not have her while she was carrying Burns's bastard. As it happened, it was bastards. Twins, Robert and Jean were born to Jean on 3 September 1786. Robert was taken by the Burns family to be brought up up at Mossgiel with Bess Paton's Elizabeth, and Jean would stay with the Armours in Mauchline. She was to die there at fourteen months in October 1787. While Jean was coping with the problems of becoming a mother for the first time, Burns was doing likewise with the business of becoming a printed poet.'

Influential friends had prevailed upon another Wilson, John, a printer in Kilmarnock (A8), to publish by subscription the 34 poems plus various epistles, epigrams and epitaphs that make up what is now called the Kilmarnock Edition. Another voyage was booked on the *Bell* and all Burns's attention was then given to publication.

> *This while my notion's ta'en a sklent*
> *To try my fate in guid, black print.*

At last he had a definite aim and a real chance to attain that thing he must have subconsciously wanted all along – fame. As Gilbert wrote – 'He was always panting after distinction'. Burns disarmingly admitted this himself: 'Obscure as I am, & obscure I must be, though no young poet, nor young soldier's heart ever beat more fondly for fame than mine.' To find it, however, he had to go to Kilmarnock.

Kilmarnock

On 31 July 1786, *Poems, Chiefly in the Scottish Dialect* was published from John Wilson's Printing Shop in Starr Inn Close at the corner of King Street. 612 subscribed copies in blue paper at three shillings a copy were sold in a matter of weeks. This was the single event that established Kilmarnock (A8) as the academic Burns HQ, the future home of the Burns Federation, the hub from where all matters of Burns interest are spoked around the world. The Kay Park Monument (built in 1879) is at its centre and houses the original Kilmarnock Edition hot from John Wilson's premises. It is, therefore, appropriate we should consider Kilmarnock as his final Ayrshire stage, as it was from here that, figuratively speaking, he went out into the world.

In the last half of the 18th century, in what is termed the Age of Enlightenment, Freemasonry, with its promise of international brotherhood and intellectual opportunity, made itself highly popular and, with its side benefits of social pleasures and material advancement, attracted many Scots, including Burns. He had joined the St David's Lodge No 174, Tarbolton, being passed and raised on 1 October 1781. This Lodge was taken over by St James, Kilwinning, and in 1784, on moving to Mossgiel, Burns was appointed Depute-Master. Burns's zeal for masonry was to diminish somewhat in later life, but the fact remains that it was a vital factor in the creation of Robert Burns, Published Author, and for that at least we must be grateful. At the Kilmarnock Kilwinning Lodge were 'the sons of old Killie assembled by Willie' – the nine Freemasons who were largely responsible for the Kilmarnock Edition of 1786. Willie was Will Parker and the others were Tam Samson, Robert Muir, John Goldie, Gavin Turnbull, Bailie Greenshields and the three doctors, Moore, Hamilton and Paterson. The printer John Wilson was a member of Lodge St John No22, which emanated from the Kilmarnock Kilwinning mother club, and it was this club which made Burns an honorary member.

Within this dear mansion, may wayward contention or withered envy ne'er enter.

*May secrecy round be the mystical bound and brotherly
love be the centre...*

It should also be noted that this was the first public honour he
ever received and the first time he was referred to officially as
'Poet Burns'. Yet however much he may have accommodated his
fellow-masons with a song, he kept a clear eye on the business in
hand. He had a poet's realistic approach to his own creations. As
he later wrote in his Autobiographical Letter in 1787:

> I weighed my productions as impartially as in my power; I thought they
> had merit; and 'twas a delicious idea that I should be thought a clever
> fellow, even though it should never reach my ears, a poor negro-driver,
> or perhaps a victim to that inhospitable clime gone to the world of the
> spirits. I can only say that as a pauvre Inconnu, as I then was, I had
> nearly as high an opinion of myself and my works as I have at this
> moment... I was pretty sure my poems would meet with some applause,
> but at the worst, the roar of the Atlantic would drown the voice of cen-
> sure, and the novelty of West Indian scenes make me forget neglect. I
> threw off 600 copies of which I had got subscriptions for about 350. My
> vanity was highly gratified by the reception I got from the general pub-
> lick, besides pocketing, all expenses deducted, near twenty pounds.

So immediate was the response to the subscriptions that a second edition was called for at once, but Printer Wilson would not
do so without the full costs in advance. Besides, he thought that
one book of poems was surely enough in anybody's life time.
Burns merely shrugged and booked a further nine-guinea passage,
this time on the *Roselle* – oddly enough now under Captain
Richard Brown.

Then, out of the blue, Burns heard from a Dr Blacklock in
Edinburgh advising him to try for a second edition there.
Edinburgh? It was almost as foreign to Robert Burns as the Indies
might have been, and in a sense, almost as far away. But why not?
Anyway, the *Roselle* was to sail out of Leith, and he had his passage booked. If a second edition didn't materialise, he would at
least be at hand to sail, and he would sail alone. Mary Campbell,
his intended companion of the voyage, had gone to await him at

the port of Greenock (A19) – but had died there. Burns, with nothing to keep him in Ayshire, had nothing to lose. So, early on the morning of 27 November 1786, on a hired horse, he set out by way of Sorn, Muirkirk and Douglas. After a convivial detour to meet admirers at Covington Mains Farm at Thankerton, he continued next morning through the Pentland Hills and along the Water of Leith, passing the villages of Currie, Balerno and Colinton, and he entered Edinburgh by the old east gate of the capital. He had to dismount and walk his horse through the crowded streets to the stables in the Grassmarket. Then, lifting his bag on to his shoulder, he went to seek out his old friend, John Richmond.

CHAPTER 2

Edinburgh

(27 November 1786 to 5 May 1787)

Edina! Scotia's darling seat!
All hail thy palaces and tow'rs...

THERE IS NO DOUBT THAT Edinburgh must have been something of a culture shock to Burns. However much the spiral of his worldly acquaintance might have extended from Tarbolton (A5) through Irvine (A6) to Kilmarnock (A8), nothing could have prepared the country boy for his first glimpse of the spilling mass that clung to the rock around Edinburgh Castle. The city at that time huddled either side of the spine of the Royal Mile which ran from the Lawnmarket down to Holyroodhouse. The New Town was then being built, but Edinburgh was still that dense conurbation of tall tenements, or lands, that comprised the Old Town, and it was here, in the Grassmarket, that Burns found himself on the evening of 28 November 1786.

In addition to the ordinary tensions of being a stranger in the big city, Burns was also feeling the strains of the journey itself. Making his solitary way across the wide waist of Scotland, he was taken aback by how well he was already known outside Ayrshire. An overnight halt had been arranged at the Prentice farm near Thankerton as part of the horse-hire arrangement and this became the excuse for an all-night party, as farmers from all over the district hurried to the Prentice place to shake the hand of the Ayrshire Bard.

He had made about 50 pounds from the Kilmarnock Edition, but more than half of that had been left with Gilbert and the family at Mossgiel, so Burns could not afford to act the gentleman. He arranged to share a room in Baxter's Close (B1) in the Lawnmarket with his friend, John Richmond, from Mauchline (A7). Richmond rented his accommodation from Mrs Carfrae for three shillings a week, and for half of that Burns had a part-use of 'a deal table, a sanded floor and a chaff bed'. It was minimal but it was adequate. Burns was so overwhelmed by this sudden cata-pulting into the metropolis, that he stayed in Richmond's room for two days before venturing out. Eventually, however, he had to make the effort, and he stepped out into the street.

Then out into the world, my course I did determine
Tho' to be rich I did not wish,
Yet to be great was charming...

Thanks to his Masonic contacts, he had a whole bundle of introductory letters in his pocket. It was now time to use them.

Sir John Whitefoord had been master of the Tarbolton Lodge while he lived at Ballochmyle, and he passed Burns on, with com-pliments, to another Ayrshire brother, Dalrymple of Orangefield, who in turn, introduced him to James Cunningham, the 14th Earl of Glencairn – and suddenly all doors were opened. He had only been in Edinburgh a week. Professor Dugald Stewart, who had

actually read the Kilmarnock Edition, saw to it that it was reviewed very favourably by Henry Mackenzie in *The Lounger*, a maga-zine published by a William Creech, and Burns had found his publisher. Once again, nine men rallied round. This time, Henry Erskine, Dr Hugh Blair and Ramsay of Ochtertyre joined those men-tioned above, and a second edition was put in hand with Creech. It can be seen that Burns was no slouch at net-working. The incidence of nine in Burns's life is of a small passing interest here. In addition to these nine men involved in

Anchor Close

the Edinburgh Edition of 1787, we had the pre-vious nine of Killie, and when the first Burns Supper was held in Alloway in the summer of 1801, at the instigation of John Ballantine, and organised by the Rev Hamilton Paul, there were nine men present. The others were Robert Aiken, Patrick Douglas,

Primrose Kennedy, Hew Ferguson, David Scott, Thomas Jackson and William Crawford. The poet was born in 1759, grew to 5'9" and held that 'nine inches will please a lady'. At any rate, he had nine children by Jean Armour – Robert, Jean, Francis, William, Elizabeth, James and Maxwell, and girl twins who died soon after birth in March 1788.

When Creech arranged for the printing to be done at Smellie's Printing Shop in Anchor Close (B3), off the High Street (B4), the young poet met Smellie and, in doing so, made his first real Edinburgh friend. Burns gave a glimpse of him in *The Poet's Progress*:

His uncomb'd, hoary locks, wild-staring, thatched
A head for thought profound and clear unmatch'd;
Yet tho' his caustic wit was biting rude
His heart was warm, benevolent and good.

William Smellie was a brilliant man. His broad knowledge of literature and science enabled him to become the editor and principle author of the very first edition of the *Encyclopaedia Britannica*. He also wrote *A Philosophy of Natural History*. So this was no ordinary printer, and certainly a change from John Wilson. Smellie had printed Robert Fergusson before Burns, so he was no stranger to poets. He and Burns took to each other from the start, and before long, Burns was seated on a high stool in the corner correcting proofs. Diligently he went through each line for the printer, discussing with him what should go in and what come out. Burns was being given a second chance and he took it. This was how he spent his days. His nights, however, were spent in a very different manner, although pursued just as diligently. For by chance or mischance, 'that old veteran in genius, wit and bawdry', Willie Smellie, was also founder of the Crochallan Fencibles – a body of men raised in those pseudo-patriotic times, less to serve their country than to serve themselves.

The Fencibles was really an excuse for like-minded gentlemen to meet in Dawney Douglas's Tavern in the same Anchor Close as the print-shop to drink and bandy words. Their name came from the landlord's singing of his favourite Gaelic song, *Cro Chalein*, and also perhaps from the company's habit of crossing swords verbally on almost every subject. Singing and debating was encouraged as long as it didn't interfere too much with drinking. Burns, remembering his Tarbolton Bachelors' Club times, delighted in this sort of mock-military evening and the chance it gave for banter and witty exchange, although he says he was bested by Smellie on most occasions.

Edinburgh High Street, looking east

No doubt, it was in this same spirit of raillery that Burns delivered for the members his *Ode to a Haggis*:

> *Fair fa' your honest, sonsy face*
> *Great chieftain of the pudding race!*
> *Weel are you wordy of a grace*
> *As long's my airm...*

This harmless bit of fun, so obviously satirical in its mock-seriousness, has somehow enshrined itself as near Holy Writ within the liturgy of the traditional Burns Supper and is presented solemnly by its reciter as if it were one of his great works. Burns's tongue was obviously in his cheek even if his hand was on his heart. This veneration of a plain dish is quite in keeping with the spirit of the Crochallans and it should be received as such and no more. The haggis itself, made as it is from the odds and ends of a sheep, doesn't entice even as a dish, yet it is extremely tasty. It is defined as having the heart, lungs, liver, chitterlings and smaller intestines of the sheep minced with suet and oatmeal and seasoned with salt, pepper and onions and all boiled like a sausage in the paunch or stomach of the sheep. It sounds awful, but it isn't. Served with neeps (turnips) and a dram of whisky, it's delicious.

Its origins are obscure. The dish, as we know it, was brought to Scotland by Mary Queen of Scots' French chef in 1561 and has remained popular with Scots ever since. The recipe was never printed, however, until it appeared in *Cookery and Pastry* by Mrs McIver in 1787, a year after Burns himself first recited his *Ode* in Edinburgh. The Ode was printed in the December issue of the *Caledonian Mercury* (the first time any poem by Burns had appeared in a newspaper).

It also appeared in the *Scots Magazine* of January 1787. Not bad for a little thing thrown off as a piece of foolery. Today, to show the lasting effect of the cult, Scots are even called 'Haggis' by non-Scots. Such is fame.

> I am in a fair way to becoming as eminent as Thomas a Kempis or John Bunyan and you may expect henceforth to see my birthday in the Poor Robin's or Aberdeen Almanacks along with Black Monday and the Battle of Bothwell Bridge... My subscription bills come out tomorrow.

Burns's reference to his own sudden fame might have been jocular, but it was certainly accurate. His appearance at the Duchess of Gordon's salon caused him to be dubbed 'the wonder of all the gay world' by Mrs Patrick Cochrane, and there is no doubt about the stir he had caused in Edinburgh society. Dressed in his famous blue with the buff waistcoat, high boots and lace at his neck and cuffs, the Mauchline dandy had come into his own. Even before his book came out he had been toasted by the Grand Master at a meeting of all the Grand Lodges of Scotland as 'Caledonia's Bard – Brother Burns!' which Burns said –

> rang through the whole assembly with multiplied honours and repeated acclamations. As I had no idea such a thing would happen, I was downright thunder struck, and trembling in every nerve made the best return in my power. Just as I finished, some of the Grand Masters said so loud as I could hear... 'Very well indeed,' which set me something to rights again.

Burns met everyone who was anyone in Edinburgh in that first year except James Boswell. Boswell was, in fact, an Ayrshire neighbour of Burns, his family estate of Auchinleck being only a few miles from Mossgiel, but the two men had never met, the distance between their stations in life being much more than the mere miles of rural roadway. When Burns came to Edinburgh, Boswell was in London, and when Boswell returned to Edinburgh, Burns had gone to Dumfries. One wonders what a picture of Burns from Boswell's pen might have been. Burns, however, saw Boswell's house at James Court, which had also been occupied by David Hume, the philosopher, and from where Boswell had set out, in the previous year, to tour the Highlands with Dr Johnson.

The only person in Edinburgh not to be impressed by Burns appears to have been Henry Dundas, the Solicitor-General and son of Lord President Dundas, on whose death Burns had written 'some elegiac verses, hastily composed, and rather commonplace... but his Solicitorship never took the smallest notice'. Burns had a noted capacity for choosing his enemies wisely. He discomfited many. 'That staring fellow,' Sir John Dalrymple had remarked. Not that this worried Burns in 1787.

The Second Edition came out – 'the whole I have printed is three thousand' – to an even better reception than the first. As a consequence, he had Edinburgh at his feet – 'never did four shillings purchase so much friendship since Confidence went first to market, or Honesty was set to sale'. Rather impetuously, he sold the copyright outright to Creech for one hundred pounds 'to be payable on demand', but it took more than six months to get the money out of that tight-fisted publisher. While Burns waited, he dallied, and for Burns that was dangerous. He also had his own words to answer for. In order to sell his book in the right quarters, particularly to the

gentlemen of the Caledonian Hunt, he had played up, rather too much it must be said, the image of the 'heaven-taught ploughman'. This being so, much of his instant fame in society was made up of little more than trivial curiosity and novelty. This was to prove something of a handicap when he tried to put himself on an equal footing with the gentry and My Lords. Even though he might attend as the star of Creech's frugal salons at his bookshop in the Luckenbooth, a rendezvous which Lord Monboddo called

Robert Fergusson's grave in Canongate churchyard,

'the natural resort of lawyers, authors and all sorts of literary allies', and meet easily with an even more select group at Monboddo's fortnightly 'learned suppers' at his house in the Canongate (B5), Burns was always aware of the glass wall between them and himself. This was even more obvious with the ladies.

Elizabeth Burnett (Monboddo's daughter) of the Canongate, Jane Ferrier of George Street, and Isabella Farquhar of Princes Street, were only a few of the eligible maids who delighted him and to whom he sent verses. Although these literary and other courtly attentions to them were received politely, he was always kept at a distance. His letters, too, did not elicit the kind of reply he hoped for, and some, like Miss Alexander, did not even bother to reply when he wrote to her:

> Poets are such outré beings, so much the children of wayward fancy and capricious whim, that I believe the world allows them a larger latitude in the laws of propriety than the sober sons of judgement and prudence.

Such a line is not guaranteed to impress a young lady – whatever her station. Small wonder then that our poet fell back to a lesser and more congenial level of female company. Burns may have had to accept a share of John Richmond's bed at Mrs Carfrae's (B2), but from time to time other bedmates beckoned. After all, comfort was nearer at hand for the two young men than the pious Mrs Carfrae preferred to admit. Burns wrote at the time:

Mrs Carfrae's tenement, now the Writers' Museum

> She is at present in sore tribulation respecting some 'Daughters of Belial' who are on the floor immediately above.' The proximity of a brothel within reach was no doubt too great a temptation. How often must the friends have lain and listened to what was going on. Likewise Mrs Carfrae, in her hard widow's cot. She told Burns that 'we should not be uneasy and envious because the Wicked enjoy the good

things of life', but at 28 years of age Burns wasn't so sure.

The nature of tenement life in Edinburgh at that time meant that in any building one would find everyone from a Lord to a laddie or Her Ladyship to the tart, and everything in between. Every house was one of ill-fame and proprietry at the same time and, as at Mrs Carfrae's, the bawdy house was only a few beams and an inch or so of plaster away from the Godly home of the Righteous. Good and Evil lived as neighbours and neither seemed to be the better or the worse for it.

May Cameron was described as a servant girl, but the service she provided was appreciated by more than her various employers. She was to claim that Robert Burns was the father of her child. This was not impossible, and in the days prior to blood tests it was not possible to prove, but Burns took the blame and sent her ten shillings via Bob Ainslie, a lawyer friend. He knew the father might have been any one of a number of men. So did May, but that didn't stop her, a year later, pursuing him to Dumfries with a writ of *meditatione fugae*. Nothing is known of the child that was born to May Cameron.

His stay in Edinburgh, however, happily bore other fruits for Robert Burns, two of which were to have life-long effects – a commission in the Excise and the informal editorship of the *Scottish Musical Museum*. The first was put into his head by his surgeon friend, Sandy Wood, as an alternative to farming or even as a co-occupation. Despite his great success so far, it had become obvious to Burns that man could not live by poetry alone – or at least, live comfortably – and he had what he called 'a life-rented horror of farming'. Anything was preferable to a farm. One well-meaning admirer (Mrs Dunlop of Dunlop) suggested that he might think of buying a commission in the army with his book money but that idea didn't attract. The idea of going forward with the Excise suggestion was entirely his own. It was a secure Government appointment with enough excitement in it to stimulate and not enough to agitate. With the perks it offered and the chance of travel throughout Scotland, Burns thought its prospects good enough to consider settling down with a wife somewhere, if he could find one. Jean Armour was there. Jean would always be there, he knew that, even if she were, at the moment, exiled to Paisley (A20), but something in him hankered after different aims than domesticity. Even though he knew that:

> To make a happy, fireside clime for weans and wife
> That's the true pathos and sublime of human life...

He would always write. He could never not. But he knew too that he had to work to live. The question was, at what? Farmer or exciseman? Either would do if it could be made to pay and leave something for Gilbert and the family still at home at Mossgiel. And also leave him time and energy to write, for that was the nub of it. He could even be all three at once – poet, farmer and exciseman. Meantime, the first priority was to get his book money – or part of it at least – from Creech. Then it would be time to make decisions.

Before he went to Edinburgh, there is no evidence that Burns ever saw a play, yet one of the first friends he made there was the actor, William Wood, an Englishman and the darling of the first Theatre Royal in the Canongate (B7). Woods arranged that Burns be given a free pass, a courtesy he had done for Edinburgh's own poet, Robert Fergusson, the decade before. Burn's admiration for this tragic young legal clerk and poet/playwright was immense and stated in print long before he ever came to Edinburgh himself.

> O, Fergusson! Thy glorious parts
> Ill-suited law's dry dusty arts
> My curse upo' your whinstane hearts,
> Ye E'nbro' gentry!
> The tythe o' what ye waste at cartes
> Wad stowed his pantry!

Fergusson's pauper grave in the Canongate Kirkyard was one of the first places Burns visited in Edinburgh. It was unmarked by any stone, so Burns petitioned the magistrates to erect one at his own expense. This was done, but it took Burns four years to pay for it. When Mr Burn, the architect/stonemason, complained and wanted to charge interest, Burns retorted that since it took the man two years to do the job, Burns was justified in waiting two years to pay him. He also added that since it was money owed by one poet for putting a stone over another, he was lucky to see a penny of it. Mr Burn replied saying he would be happy to put a gravestone over Burns, or any of his friends, at any time.

Had Fergusson lived beyond his 24 years, he would surely have met up with Burns in Edinburgh. What a combustible combination they might have made at the theatre or in a salon. They might have joined their mutual admiration for William Wallace and finished the play Fergusson had started on that Scottish hero. Fergusson was a member of the Cape Club, yet another drinking excuse for gentlemen of wit and capacity, but what the two had most in common was that sense of Scottish *gravitas* in their better work. By their use of old Scotch in their poetry they went some way to saving an ancient tongue. They were East and West of Scotland and what a pity they never met, for their twin voices resonate yet with a vibrant Scottishness that was well able to resist the tide of Englishness that came with the Enlightenment.

Alexander Nasmyth was another bosom companion found in the Edinburgh drinking clubs. He was to paint the original Burns

portrait which is the basis of the thousand and one ubiquitous images of the poet that survive today. When Creech asked Nasmyth to paint the poet for the frontispiece of the editions of Burns that were to pour out from this time on, Naysmyth was delighted to do so free of charge, so much did he admire his sitter. Needless to say, Mr Creech was even more delighted and, as a result, the world has the Burns portrait that has come to be the accepted traditional likeness. Nasmyth also shared Burns's egalitarian views, not an entirely safe view to have in the Edinburgh of that time. Burns never hesitated about making his political attitude known, but

Lady Stair's Close

he tried to be prudent for the most part. He knew he 'was in a new world' and that he 'mingled among many classes of men' but he was 'all attention to catch the manners living as they rise'. The learning curve was steep, but he was more than equal to it.

He warmed to artists of all kinds and especially to the singers and musicians. Stephen Clarke was a music teacher and he had been brought in to work as an arranger on a publishing project with James Johnson (B8). Johnson was a musical printer and engraver in Lady Stair's Close (B2) off the Lawnmarket. He had invented a method of reproducing sheet music on pewter plates and had used it to publish in that year the first volume of the *Scottish Musical Museum* comprising a hundred songs. Through Clarke, Johnson approached Burns to see if he could help in the matter of lyrics. By doing this, he didn't know he was starting Burns off on his whole life's work. Burns wrote to him at once:

> Had my acquaintance with you been a little older, I would have asked the favor of your correspondence; as I have met with few people whose company & conversation gave me so much pleasure, because I have met with few whose sentiments are so congenial to my own...

The work of saving old songs was a labour of love for Burns, one that he was to undertake freely and thoroughly until the last few days of his life. He felt he could not take pay for such work. A song belonged to everybody as far as he was concerned. Far from being merely the lyric polisher for Johnson, he was virtually to become the editor and chief collector of the enterprise as the *Musical Museum* went into its further editions. The project was to catch at one of Burns's great enthusiasms, and in this work with Johnson, and later, George Thomson, he was to feel himself totally fulfilled. Unfortunately, Johnson's approach had come just as the poet was about to leave on a tour of the Borders with Bob Ainslie. Creech had come up with some cash at last and Burns resolved to spend it on a holiday – his first ever.

He had once described himself as 'a poor, wayfaring Pilgrim on the road to Parnassus; [a] thoughtless wanderer and sojourner in a strange land'. Apart from that narrow Lowland belt between Ayrshire and Edinburgh, Scotland was still a 'strange land' to him.

He resolved, as soon as he could, to remedy that. His book was now out in the world and had begun its way around it. He had money in his pocket and time to spare. He was determined to use it, for once, for leisure and pleasure. He knew he might never have the same chance again. Everything else must wait on this great adventure:

Catch the moments as they fly
And use them as ye ought, man!
Believe me, happiness is shy
And comes not aye when sought, man!

He had also written in a letter to Mrs Dunlop:

The appellation of a Scotch bard is by far my highest pride; to continue to deserve it is my highest ambition. Scottish scenes and Scottish stories are the themes I wish to sing. I have no greater, no dearer aim than to have it in my power, unplagued with the routine of business, for which, Heaven knows, I am unfit enough, to make leisurely pilgrimages through Caledonia; to sit on the fields of her battles; to wander the romantic banks of her rivers; and to muse by the stately towers or venerable ruins, once the honest abodes of her heroes – but these are Utopians ideas...

Utopian or not, they came to pass on Saturday 5 May 1787 when he set off for a tour of the Borders on his own mare, Jenny Geddes (bought for 4 pounds in the Grassmarket), together with Bob Ainslie. Ainslie, a law student and fellow-Mason, was by now his closest Edinburgh friend and ally. Burns said of him, 'You assume a proper length of face in my bitter hours of blue-devilism and you laugh fully up to my highest wishes at my good things.' Ainslie loved wine, women and song almost as much as Burns, so they were a well-matched pair as holiday companions. Ainslie's family came from the Border country and this may have suggested the route the two young men took. There was also the side-business of collecting book-monies en route from the various subscribers throughout the country. Not only would such collections finance the trip but they would also provide Burns with a much-needed cushion against what future career choice he would have to make before the end of the year. While it was principally a holiday excursion and secondly a fund-raising mission, Burns was to find to his surprise that it was also something of a royal progress.

Before setting off, he went back to Covington Mains Farm for a brief visit. For what reason, he never would say, but a certain farmer's daughter was held to be the magnet. She was to be the subject of another of his love songs, and in a letter to Gavin Hamilton, his Mauchline lawyer, he said, 'I have met with a very pretty girl, a Lothian farmer's daughter, whom I have almost persuaded to accompany me to the West Country should I ever return there...' Yet, being Burns, in the first part of the letter, or the fragment of it that remains, he confides to Hamilton his continuing feelings for Jean Armour: 'To tell truth among friends, I feel a miserable blank in my heart for want of her, and I don't think I shall ever meet with so delicious an armful again. She has her faults: and so have you and I; and so has everybody.' When pressed later about the story of the Lothian farmer's daughter, all he would say was that 'it alludes to a part of my private history, which it is of no consequence for the world to know'. So be it.

CHAPTER 3

The Borders

(5 May to 1 June 1787)

Berrywell – Duns – Coldstream – Cornhill – Kelso – Jedburgh
– Wauchope – Stodrig – Melrose – Selkirk – Innerleithen – Traquair
– Caddenfoot – Galashiels – Earlston – Gordon – Greenlaw – Berwick
– Eyemouth – Coldingham Abbey – Peasebridge – Dunbar – Dunglass
– Skateraw – Wooler – Alnwick – Warkworth – Morpeth – Newcastle
– Hexham – Wardrue – Longtown – Carlisle

Duns

THIS FIRST TRIP TO THE Border country marked Burns's debut as a celebrity. He went with a certainty that he would be stared at, pointed out, talked to, and by the same token, ignored, but he might also have been slightly uncertain about how he might react to the practicalities of fame. The Nasmyth frontispiece had gone ahead of him and he would have to live up to it. Once again he was embracing a new experience.

He had had his 'phiz done' as he termed it, and it had appeared in the first Edinburgh Edition of his poems on 21 April; now he had no less than three dozen proof-prints of the Beugo engraving in his travel-bag ready to give away to admirers if asked for. The fact that he brought them at all suggests that he had an idea of what he might be in for. It was the money from this same Edinburgh Edition, several hundred pounds at least, that subsidised his journeys.

There were to be four main tours in the travelling year of 1787, but this first one to the Borders begun on that Saturday morning in early May surely had a special excitement for him, togged up as he was in new travelling clothes. Creech's cash was already being well spent. He and Ainslie must have seemed like any other young gentlemen as they rode by. Burns's stocky farmer's 5ft 9ins was flattered on horseback. In the same way, he looked at ease seated at table. It was only when he walked that the years of labour on the farms told. It showed in his heavy tread (unusual in a good dancer) and his slightly stooped back and rounded ploughman shoulders. However, while riding, he might have been one of the gentry. This was to mislead many on the tour.

That first day, the tourists reached Berrywell (c1), the Ainslie family home near Duns (c2).

Left Edinr – Haddington – Gifford – Longformacus – Lammermuir Hills miserably dreary but at times very picturesque – Lanton Edge... reach Berrywell – old Mr Ainslie, an uncommon character...the clearest-headed, best-informed man I have ever been with – As a man of business he has uncommon merit, and by fairly deserving it has made a very decent independence – Mrs Ainslie, an excellent, sensible, cheerful, amiable old woman – Miss Ainslie an angel...

The charming Rachel Ainslie was the nearest thing to a female friend Burns was ever to know. Writing to her brother later, he asked to be remembered to 'my friend Rachel, who is as far before Rachel of old, as she was before her blear-eyed sister Leah'. He went to the local church in Duns with the family on the Sunday morning and found himself sitting with Rachel. She couldn't find in her Bible the text the minister, Dr Bowmaker, had given out, which was on sinners. While she was looking through the pages, Burns scribbled the following in his notebook and passed it to her:

Fair maid, you needna take the hint,
Nor idle texts pursue,
'Twas guilty sinners that he meant,
Not angels such as you!

Burns's gift for poetic improvisation was not always so felicitous and would land him in considerable trouble from time to time. But the tongue that got him into bother invariably got him out of it again – or his ready pen came to the rescue.

He started off with the intention of keeping a journal of his travels for later use as a resource for more considered writing but gradually the notes for the day diminished to a mere record of places and names, little more than a memory-jogger, and finally dwindled away altogether. Good writing is rarely something one does on the road, especially after a day on a horse, and in any case the pressure of events and people was such that he had little time or opportunity to collect his thoughts for a meaningful journal.

Nevertheless, what he did write was sufficient to point the reader in the right direction. In some cases, the entries were all the more intriguing for their brevity. For instance:

Monday 7th May – Coldstream (c3) – went over into England...

No more than four words for a significant invasion. After all, this was the first time Robert Burns had ever stepped on foreign soil. He had never been out of Scotland before. Ainslie told James Hogg more than fifty years later that on this signal occasion Burns had knelt down and invoked a blessing on Scotland, quoting his own work.

Be that as it may, it was hardly a toe-hold he made that afternoon on the opposite bank of the 'glorious River Tweed', and he and Ainslie returned to Coldstream, that refuge for eloping couples, to dine with a local farmer, Mr Foreman. Burns notes that he 'beat Mr F in a dispute about Voltaire'; and also, 'my reception from Mr and Mrs Bryden extremely flattering – sleep at Coldstream'.

Kelso

The journal continues:

Kelso Abbey

Tuesday 8th May – Breakfasted at Kelso (c5) – fine bridge over the Tweed – enchanting view & prospects on both sides of the river, particularly the Scotch side – visit ruins of Roxburgh Castle – A bush growing where James 2nd of Scotland was accidentally killed by the bursting of a cannon – bad roads – magnificent farm houses and fine lands not above 16 sh[illings] Scots acre – Came up the Jed to Jedburgh to lie and wish myself goodnight.

No doubt before he slept he went over the land and animal prices he had talked about with Mr McDowell of Caverton Mill, a friend of Ainslie. He also noted that the sheep were washed before shearing. Once a farmer...

Jedburgh

Wednesday 9 May – Breakfast with Mr Fair – who is blind but the first man of business as a Writer in the town. Mrs Fair, a crazy, talkative slattern and her sister (Miss Lookup) an old maid, get into an argument about the relief minister... (C6)

Burns was glad to escape the two women by going two miles out of town to attend an auction of land. He met a Captain Rutherford, an ex-soldier, who had been in America with the British Army and had been captured by the Chippewah Indians. Burns happily accepted his invitation to dine and was immediately captivated by the daughter –

Miss Rutherford a beautiful girl, but too far gone woman to expose so much of a fine, swelling bosom...

He met Mrs Fair and Miss Lookup, the sparring sisters, the next day when he and Ainslie were asked to join the ladies in an afternoon walking party to the Love-lane. The acquaintance did not improve on either side. This was because all Burns's attention was given to Miss Isabella Lindsay, 'a pretty girl, fond of laughing and fun', but the other ladies, Miss Lookup in particular, were keeping a wary eye on both of them. Shaking himself free of Mrs Fair and Miss Lookup with some difficulty, he –

somehow or other got hold of Miss Lindsay's arm - my heart thawed into melting pleasure after being so long frozen up in the Greenland Bay of Indifference amid the noise and nonsense of Edinr... The Poet is a point and a half of being damnably in love.

Just as Isabella and Burns were getting better acquainted, Miss Lookup fell on them reproachfully and abused the girl particularly for her flirtatiousness. Burns had to restrain himself from cursing her to her face as an interfering old virgin. And so to supper – but, not surprisingly, Miss Isabella did not appear at table. Burns's temper was not improved by the continued attentions of Miss Lookup. He made a point, however, of meeting Isabella Lindsay with her sister at breakfast next morning. Afterwards, taking the opportunity of walking down the garden of a friend's house with her, he discovered that his bosom 'is as tinder as ever...I find Miss Lindsay would soon play the devil with me.' He goes on:

After some little chit-chat of the tender kind, I presented her with a proof-print of my Nob which she accepted with something more tender than gratitude. She told me many little stories which Miss L had related concerning her and me, with prolonging pleasure – God bless her. Was waited on by the Magistrates and presented with the Freedom of the Burgh.

One has the feeling he would sooner have had the freedom of Miss Isabella Lindsay. It is typical of the man that he devotes a paragraph to chit-chat after breakfast and a line to a prestigious civic honour. As it happened, Burns did not even sign the Jedburgh Burgess Roll when he received his ticket. His mind must still have been on Isabella. As only three weeks later the young lady married one, Adam Armstrong, Miss Lookup may have had a point after all. (Jane Austen, who was twelve at this time and ten years away from *Sense and Sensibility*, might have made much of such a situation).

Meantime, the friends went on to meet Esther Easton, who was the gardener's wife and lived in a house on the Lindsay property, and could recite Homer and Pope from end to end but as yet knew no Burns. However, she was happy to meet with a poet 'who had put out a book' Burns and Ainslie breakfasted at Rule with Dr Gilbert Elliot, who then conveyed them to Wauchope where they met with Mrs Elizabeth Scott, who, Burns said – 'had all the sense, taste, intrepidity of face, and bold, critical decision which usually distinguish female authors'.

Kelso – dine with the Farmers' Club – all gentlemen talking of high matters go out with Mr Ker, one of the club, to lie. A most gentlemanly, clever, handsome fellow – he offers to accompany me on my English tour... Next day (12 May) devilish wet – Dine with Sir Alexander Don –

clever little fellow but far, far from being a match for his divine lady –
poverty and pride the reigning features of the family – lie at Stodrig
(C8) again – still bad weather – visit Dryburgh, a fine, old ruined Abbey
by the way...

Melrose

The days continued wet and cold and
it is little wonder that Burns
was not overly impressed
with what he saw of the
Vale of Yarrow – 'the whole
country hereabout, both on
Tweed and Ettrick, remarkably
stony'. (C9)

Melrose Abbey

Monday 14th May – Come to Inver-leithing, a famous Spaw, & and in
the vicinity of the palace of Traquair, where, having dined, and drank
some Galloway-whey, I remain till tomorrow.

Inverleithing, near Peebles, is Innerleithen (C11) today. In
Burns's time it was no more than a few thatched cottages. He
stayed at the only inn in the High Street then called the Piccadilly.
One would have thought, with his proved and often-stated
Jacobite sympathies, he would have been accommodated at
Traquair. (C12) After seeing Elibanks and Elibraes, 'so famous in
bawdy song', he and Ainslie made their way via Galashiels (C14)
to Earlston (C15), the birthplace of Thomas the Rhymer, and saw
the ruins of his castle. They then came via Ettrick to Selkirk.

Selkirk

Arriving at Veitch's Forest Inn (C10) in the pouring rain, they
found it crowded and Ainslie asked if they might join a table
which had space for two chairs, but a certain Dr Clarkson, whose
party it was, declined to have the muddied pair sit with them. He
explained that, while one 'sounded nearly like a gentlemen' the

other was 'a drover-looking chap'. When he heard next day that the 'other' was the celebrated Burns, Clarkson was mortified, as he was a genuine admirer of the poet and had his book. He went to meet him at the other inn, but Burns was in bed, drying out, feeling 'jaded to death'. He didn't see the good doctor. Ordinarily he would have done so, and with some humour, but, as he feared, he was finding it hard to be on show all the time. The poor Dr Clarkson spent the rest of his life regretting his moment of hauteur which cost him the company at dinner of one of the most famous men in Scotland. Today a plaque marks the site of the incident.

> Wednesday 16 May – dined at Duns with the Farmer's club – Company – impossible to do them justice – Rev Mr Smith, a famous punster and Mr Meikle, a celebrated Mechanic and inventor of the threshing-mill – lie again at Berrywell.

On returning to the Ainslie home, he found packets of original poetry sent to him by Symon Gray, a Londoner, now retired to Duns. Gray wanted to know Burns's honest opinion of his verses. Burns duly replied to the first package:

Symon Gray, you're dull today!

And to the second:

Dullness, wit redoubted sway, has seized the wits of Symon Gray.

And when a third bulky parcel arrived:

Dear Symon Gray, the other day,
When you sent me some rhyme,
I could not then just ascertain
Its worth for want of time.
But now today, good Master Gray,
I've read it o'er and o'er,
Tried all my skill, but find I'm still
Just where I was before.
We auld wives' minnions gie our opinions,
Solicited or no',
Then, of it's fau'ts my honest thoughts

I'll give – and here they go.
Such damn'd bombast no time that's past
Will show, or time to come,
So Symon, dear, your song I'll tear,
And with it, wipe my bum!

Nothing further has ever been heard of Symon Gray.

The episode more than shows Burns's gift for extempore verse. He was as spontaneous with *An Address to the Haggis* and would be so again in *The Selkirk Grace*. These little asides and the excerpts from the journal hint at a grasp of character and scene that would have served him well as a playwright. He had an unerring eye for the original and eccentric in what he saw around him in his travels – and also for what was sham.

Berwick

Friday 18th May – Via Manderston, Chirnside, Foulden, Edrington, Mordington and Halidon Hill to Berwick – an idle town, but rudely picturesque – meet Lord Errol in walking round the walls – His Lordship's flattering notice of me [Burns always loved a lord] – dine with Mr Clunzie, Mercht. – nothing particular in company or conversation – come up a bold shore & over a wild country via Burnmouth to Eyemouth – sup & sleep at Mr Grieve's.

Legend grew up that Burns did not like Berwick (c18) but there is no proof of this in his journal or in recorded incident.

Eyemouth

Saturday 19th May – spend the day at Mr Grieve's – made a royal arch Mason of St Ebbe's Lodge...

The Eyemouth Lodge (c19) considered Burns a very distinguished visitor indeed. They did not even charge him the usual fee, and the cutlery and utensils he used at the 'repast' have been kept to this day. The minute for 19 May 1787 reads:

At a general encampment held this day, the following brethren were made Royal Arch Masons, viz: Robert Burns from the Lodge of St James, Tarbolton, Ayrshire and Robert Ainslie, from the Lodge of St Luke's, Edinburgh...Robert Ainslie paid one guinea admission dues...Robert Burns admit. gratis.

After this, Ainslie's holiday time was over and he had to go back to his law practice with Samuel Mitchelson in Edinburgh. Burns carried on alone through Coldingham Abbey (c20) to Peasebridge (c21) – with some unexpected results.

Peasebridge

Here, on the evening of 21 May, Burns dined with George Sherriff – 'a crashing bore, talkative and conceited' – who had a sister, Nancy. Sherriff was suddenly called away on some business, leaving Burns alone for the rest of the evening with the sister. Fortunately, brother George returned just in time. Next morning as Burns was saddling up, to his astonishment Nancy appeared 'as fine as hands could make her, in cream-coloured riding clothes, hat and feather – to accompany him to Dunbar. Burns gave a description of the journey and of his new travel-mate in a letter to Ainslie:

> In the words of the Highlandman when he saw the Devil on Shanter-hill in the shape of five swine – 'My hair stood and my pintle stood and I swat and trembled' – Nothing could prevail with her, no distant insinuation, no broad hint would make her give over her purpose (to make a parade of me as a sweetheart of hers among her relations); at last, vexed, disgusted and enraged, I pretended a fire-haste and rode so hard she was almost shaken to pieces on old Jolly, and, to my great joy, she found it convenient to stop at an uncle's house by the way. I refused to call with her, and so we quarreled and parted.

Flirtation with pretty women, as he often declared, was just his kind of sport, but every now and then it backfired. It was a game played in a social context and it was expected, on both sides, that it end with the end of the evening. Few of the ladies were as determined as Nancy Sherriff. Once he had escaped, he made his way through 'the most glorious corn country I ever saw' till he reached Dunbar (D1), 'a neat little town'.

Dunbar

Here, he dined with the Provost and called on Miss Clarke – 'a maiden, in the Scotch phrase, guid enough but no' brent new'. According to Burns's journal entry,

> She wanted to see what rare show an Author was; and to let him know that though Dunbar was but a little town yet it was not destitute of people of parts.

He left Dunbar (D1) for Dunglass (C22) and had breakfast next morning at Skateraw (C23) with Mr Lee,

> a farmer of great note and an excellent, hospitable, social fellow – comp. at dinner – my revd acquaintance, Dr Bowmaker, a revd, rattling, rattling, drunken old fellow – two sea Lieutenants; a Mr D. Lee, a cousin of the landlord's, a fellow whose looks are of that kind which deceived me in a gentleman at Kelso, and has often deceived me; a goodly, handsome figure and face which incline one to give them credit for parts which they have not... Mr Lee detains me till next morning...

Burns left for Duns with Charles Lorimer, the Collector of Excise at Dunbar. One wonders if Burns aired his ideas about his own Commisssion, but this is unlikely in view of Burns's comment on Lorimer. He said that he was – 'a lad of slender abilities and bashfully indifferent to an extreme...' Nevertheless, Lorimer spent a long life in the Excise and retired on a comfortable pension until his death in 1824, something Burns himself would dearly have liked, and indeed, hoped for.

On arriving at the Ainslie home at Berrywell (C1), he found Rachel awaiting him. There was no one else at home and Burns found himself alone with her in the house. He was enchanted with her. 'Miss Ainslie – the amiable, sweet, the sensible, the good-humoured, the sweet Miss Ainslie, all alone at Berrywell...' The two had dinner together – 'how well-bred, how frank, how good she is'. There was no banter, no flirtation here, although he did note later, 'I could grasp her with rapture on a bed of straw'. Burns was at his gentlemanly best. There was no sport to be had with his best friend's sister. This was no 'piece'. Rachel Ainslie was in a different class altogether from Nancy Sherriff. He went on, 'Charming Rachel!

May thy bosom never be wrung by the evils of this life of sorrows, or by the villainy of this world's sons.' His prayer was answered. She was only nineteen at this time, and although she lived long, she never married, and preferred to live quite happily at home. Burns never lost his admiration for her, but he always kept his distance, an unusual stance for him. She was a friend. Strangely, he never 'made a song upon her'. Perhaps, for the first time on the tour, Burns was able to be himself with a woman.

> Thursday 24th May – Mr Ker and I set out for to dine at Mr Hood's (C24) on our way to England – 'I am taken extremely ill with feverish symptoms, and take a servant of Mr Hood's to watch me all night – embittering remorse scares my fancy at the gloomy forebodings of death. I am determined to live for the future in such a manner as not to be scared at the approach of Death – I am sure I could meet him with indifference, but for The Something beyond the grave – Mr Hood agrees to accompany us to England if we will wait him till Sunday.

Alnwick

And so, on Sunday 27 May, Burns once again crossed the Tweed and after coming through 'a wild country' reached Alnwick (C25), the seat of the Duke of Northumberland.

> A Mr Wilkinson, an agent of His Grace's showed us through Alnwick Castle... furnished in a most princely manner... Mr W a discreet, sensible, ingenuous man.'
> Monday 28th May – Come, still through byways to Warkworth (C26) where we dine... sleep at Morpeth (C27), a pleasant little town and on next day to Newcastle – meet with a very agreeable sensible fellow, a Mr Chattox, a Scotchman, who shows us many civilities and who dines and sups with us –

Tuesday 29 May is deleted.

Newcastle

One can only wonder what happened in Newcastle (C28). Local story has it that during dinner with Mr Chattox, Burns was rather surprised to see the meat served before the soup. Chattox explained with a laugh that there was a Northumbrian maxim which states that in these parts 'we must eat beef before we sup the broth, lest the hungry Scots make an inroad and snatch it'! He only stayed one night in Newcastle but he took time to write to James Johnson in Edinburgh, enclosing an extra verse for a song he had seen in the first volume of the *Musical Museum*. He wrote:

...These lines will set to the tune better thus than as they are printed. To the song in the first Volume, Here awa there awa, must be added this verse, the best in the song –

Gin ye meet my love, kiss her & clap her,
And gin ye meet my love, dinna think shame;
Gin ye meet my love, kiss her and clap her,
And shew her the way to haud awa hame.

There is room on the plate [Burns here means the printing plate] for it. For the tune of the Scotch queen, in Oswald; take the two first, and the two last stanzas of the Poem entitled, The Lament, in the Poems –

The blude-red rose at yule may blaw,
The simmer lilies bloom in snaw,
The frost may freeze the deepest seas,
But an auld man shall never daunton me.
Chorus:
To daunton me, to daunton me,
An auld man shall never daunton me –

The chorus is set to the first part of the tune, which just suits it, when once play'd or sung over...'

It is good to see in these instructions to Johnson that his mind was still running on work, even when he is supposed to be on holiday, although, as has been said, he never regarded anything to do with songs as work. You can be sure that as he rode along, songs and rhyming schemes would be running in his head. It is also significant that while in England for the first time in any real sense, he thinks in Scots. It was almost as if it were a reaction to his being in foreign parts. Like most expatriates, he was more Scottish out of Scotland than in it.

Longtown

Meantime, having left Newcastle early, the three horsemen crossed the North of England via Hexham (C29) and Wardrue Spa (C30), and arrived at Longtown (C31). It was hiring day there and Burns was 'uncommonly happy to see so many young folks enjoying life'. The three companions dined after Messrs Hood and Ker had completed their business, and then they parted – the farmers to return to Scotland and Burns to go to Carlisle (C32).

Carlisle

Burns lodged at the Malt Shovel Inn in the Rickergate before going out to meet Mr Mitchell, the printer, and to walk with him around the town. There is a story that the two men were separated by the crowds in the market square and Burns, knowing that they were to dine at a certain inn, made his way there. Not seeing Mitchell in the public bar, he put his head round the door of a room where some men were engaged in a private party. Not seeing him there, Burns withdrew his head at once, but a voice called out, 'Come in, Johnny Peep!' Burns joined the party and in no time he was as merry as they. Part of their fun was that each man should write a rhyme and put it with half-a-crown under the candlestick on the table. Needless to say, Burns with his entry won the contest – and the half-crowns. Here it is.

> *Here am I, Johnny Peep,*
> *I saw three sheep,*
> *And these three sheep saw me;*
> *Half-a-crown a-piece*
> *Will pay for their fleece,*
> *And so, Johnny Peep gets free.*

Even if the story is apocryphal, it's still good fun. Another doubtful anecdote connected with his Carlisle stay concerns his horse. It seems that when Burns eventually got back to the Malt Shovel Inn, rather worse for wear, the landlord, Peter Reid, told him that Jenny Geddes had been impounded for straying on to Corporation land called the Bitts, and being found grazing unlawfully there. In order to get his mare back, Burns had to report the next morning to the Town Hall pay a fine to the Mayor. He did so, but with this verse attached –

Was e'er poet sae befitted,
The maister drunk, the horse committed.
Puir harmless beast! tak' thee nae care,
Thou'lt be a horse when he's nae mair.

True or not, the story's worth the pun.

What is true, however, is that Burns took an incident that happened in England to inspire his only letter in broad Scots. It was addressed to an Edinburgh friend, William Nicol, the Latin Master at the High School, who resolutely held out in his defiant Scots vernacular against the increasing 'Englishness' of Edinburgh speech. Burns knew the schoolmaster would appreciate the 'auld Scotch tongue'. It shows Burns's extraordinary command of language, which he could put to the service of any literary need, Scots or English, and he does so here with verve and dash. In the letter he claims to be drunk, which he often does, more from effect than candour, but even if he were, he writes here with a true voice of old Scotland. It is fiercely uncompromising because he knew it was a voice that was already disappearing in his own lifetime. For this reason, no translation is offered. It deserves to be 'sounded out' with relish.

'Carlisle – 1st June 1787 – or, I believe, the 39th o' May rather...

Kind, honest-hearted Willie,

I'm setting' doon here, efter seevin an' forty miles ridin', e'en as forgesket an' forniaw'd as ae forfoughten cock, tae gie ye some notion o' my landlowper-like stravaugin' sin the sorrowfu' hoor that I sheuk hauns an' pairted wi' Auld Reekie. I hae daunder'd owre a' the kintra frae Dunbar tae Selcraig, an' hae foregaither'd

wi' mony a guid fallow, an' mony a weel-far'd hizzie - I met wi'
twa dink quines in particular, ane o' them a sonsie, fine, fodgel
lass, baith baw an' bonie; the tither wis ae clean-shank, straight,
tight, weel-far'd winch, as blithe's a lintwhite oan a flow'rie thorn,
an' as sweet an' modest's new-blawn plumrose on a hazel shaw.
They were baith bred tae mainners by the buik, an' ony ane o'
them had as muckle smeddum an' rummelgumption as the hauf o'
some presbytries you an' I baith ken. The played me sic a deevil o'
a shavie that I daursay if my harrigals were turn'd oot, ye wad see
twa nicks I' the hert o' me like the mark o' kail-white in ae cas-
tock. I was gaun te write ye a lang pystle, but, Gof forgie me, I gat
mysel' sae notouriously bitchify'd the day efter kail-time that I can
haurdly stiter but an' ben...I'll be in Dumfries the morn gif the
beast be to the fore and the branks bide hale...'

This meant he would be back in Scotland in the morning if
Jenny Geddes was up to time and the bridle held. It did, and he was.

What strikes one is how eager Burns was to get out of
England. It's rather odd that he thought to make nothing of this
experience other than write two little verses and one long letter –
and all in Scots – while he was there. Having the money, he could
easily have gone to London, as James Boswell had done, but he
never even thought about it. He had had several journalistic offers
to go there, but he hardly even considered them. He preferred to
discover his own country. Burns seemed to have an aversion to
most things English, except its literature. When, in the spring of
1790, his younger brother, William, then 23, prepared to move to
London from Newcastle on completing his apprenticeship as a
saddler, Burns was to write to him from Ellisland:

Now that you are setting out for that place... one or two things let me
particularize to you – London swarms with worthless wretches who
prey on their fellow-creatures' thoughtlessness or inexperience. Be cautious in forming connections with comrades or companions – You can
be pretty good company to yourself & you cannot be too shy of letting
anybody know you farther than as a Sadler. Another caution... Bad
Women – it is an impulse the hardest to be restrained...Whoring is a most
ruinous expensive species of dissipation...

Burns goes on to expound on the horrors of sexual diseases to the young man, something, incidentally, which never troubled Burns himself, showing that, if he dallied, he did not do so indiscriminately. He ends his letter:

Write me as soon as you reach London...and if you are in a strait for a little ready cash, you know my direction – I shall not see you beat, while you fight like a man.

The easy-going young brother had neither Robert's fire nor Gilbert's dull steadiness, and he rather fell into whatever came up for him. It was Burns who found him employment as a saddler, first at Longtown (C31) then in Newcastle. In a further letter, he offered him his own favourite couplet as a comfort in his new life.

Whether doing, suffering or forbearing
We may do miracles by persevering.
What makes the hero great is never to despair...

In a further brief letter, dated 16 July, he had found a way of introducing William to John Murdoch, Burns's old teacher from Alloway (A1), who was then in London, but it was too late. The friend who delivered the letter on Burns's behalf found William dead in his lodgings – 'of a putrid fever'. Shades of Mary Campbell. Burns, who was more a father than a brother to William, was deeply shocked and was convinced that London had killed him. This episode shows another side of Burns. Here was a man who cared for his family and for his blood – on whatever side of the blanket it came. He had in him all the qualities of the genuine paterfamilias, although he himself was not to live long enough to show it.

For the moment, however, on 2 June 1787, he crossed the border and came via Sark (A21) into Annan (A22). He was back in Scotland again. He was home and the journal abruptly ends. But the journey goes on...

CHAPTER 4

Return to the West

(1 June - 7 August 1787)

Sark – Annan – Dumfries – Dalswinton – Lochmaben – Moffat
– Thornhill – New Cumnock – Mauchline – Kilmarnock
– Glasgow – (Greenock) – Inveraray – Crocharibus – Arrochar
– Tarbert – Arden – Bannachra – Balloch – Dumbarton
– Paisley – Mauchline.

O, Scotia! my dear, my native soil...

Dumfries

IN SCOTLAND AGAIN AFTER A month of steady travelling, Burns
was back on home ground and visibly relaxed. And he was back
to his old self. He was in Dumfries (A23) by the first of the month
and seemed to make friends almost at once.

> I am quite charmed by Dumfries folk – Mr Burnside, the clergyman, in
> particular, is a man I shall ever gratefully remember; and his wife, God
> forgive me, I had almost broke the tenth commandment on her account
> – Simplicity, elegance, good sense, sweetness of disposition, good
> humour, kind hospitality are the constituents of her manner and heart; in
> short – if I say but one more word about her, I shall be in directly in love
> with her.

Anne Burnside was indeed a beauty and Burns wasn't the first
to be smitten, but she was very happy as the minister's wife.

On 4 June, he was awarded an Honorary Freedom of
Dumfries, 'gratis'. A previous recipient of this honour four years
earlier had been Patrick Miller of Dalswinton (A24) whom Burns
was now on his way to see. Burns also received at this time the
unwelcome letter from May Cameron. How she knew where to
find him and to know his date of arrival in Dumfries is something

of a mystery, unless it had been forwarded by Gilbert from Mossgiel. The letter, dated 26 May, had been written for May by someone else and in it she did not claim that Burns was the father, but that she was 'writing out of quarters, with no friends'. She wanted Burns to help find her a place 'till such time as you come to town yourself'. Burns lost no time in passing the letter on to Bob Ainslie:

Burns Statue, Dumfries

> My first welcome to this place is the inclosed letter – I am very sorry for it, but what is done is done... please call at the James Hog mentioned and send for the wench and give her ten or twelve shillings, but don't for Heaven's sake meddle with her as a piece – I insist on this, on your honour...

Burns's advice was timely in this as Bob himself had not long before got a young girl into trouble. Burns later welcomed him into 'The venerable Society of FATHERS!' and quoted no less than the Psalms in his case for illegitimate offspring –

Love's children are God's heritage;
The womb's fruit his reward;
The sons of youth as arrows are
In strong man's hands prepar'd

He also joked about May Cameron's bringing him 'half-a-Highlander'. In fact, nothing is known about the child or whether in fact it ever was born. She may have miscarried, which was common enough in her circumstances, but by August of that year, Burns was freed of her writ and nothing more was heard of May Cameron. During June, however, his thoughts were less on the making of life than on making a living, and to that end he had made an appointment to see Patrick Miller at Dalswinton.

Dalswinton

At this time, Miller was engaged on his estate in making some experiments in agricultural production methods – inventing a drill plough and a new threshing machine and feeding his cattle on steamed potatoes. His most striking project, however, was his idea for a steam-driven paddle boat, an idea which was to come to pass with William Symington's steamboat, which Miller financed. This then was the man who next came into Burns's life. He had first done so in Edinburgh at the end of Burns's first visit there when he left ten guineas for the poet. Miller was interested in Burns taking over the farm at Dalswinton (A24), but Burns was not so sure. Miller insisted that it was a bargain. Burns agreed it was a bargain – 'but one that may ruin me'. He had had his farmer's fingers burnt before. They both decided to leave matters for the time being, although that didn't stop Burns having a trip round Dalswinton Loch on the prototype steam paddle boat.

> *Marjorie of the many Lochs*
> *A Carlin auld and teugh...*

This reference in *The Five Carlins* is to another loch at Lochmaben (A25), where Marjorie Bruce the only child of Robert the Bruce, once lived in its castle. Lochmaben is an ancient royal burgh in the Annandale parish and only about eight miles from Dumfries (A23). The *Five Carlins* Burns referred to in his poem are the five burghs of Dumfriesshire, the others being Dumfries itself, Kirkudbright (A33), Annan (A22) and Sanquhar (A27). Burns always claimed that he had been given the freedom of Lochmaben after leaving Dalswinton but there is no trace of this in the official records. He may have been alluding to his Freedom ceremony earlier at Dumfries, although, in his excuse, he had received so many honorary 'freedoms' on his tours that year, it is likely they developed into a kind of burgess blur. Actually, he received six in all, if we count Lochmaben, the others being Jedburgh (C6), Dumfries, Dumbarton (A18), Linlithgow (D5) and Sanquhar. His other honours were Masonic.

He continued his journey by way of Moffat (A26), Thornhill

(A28) and New Cumnock. He stayed overnight at the last place, although it was hardly a morning's ride into Mauchline (A7). It

Burn's Cairn, New Cumnock

was if he were bracing himself for his homecoming. After so much 'noise' on the journey, perhaps he felt he needed a pause before facing his own again. After all, it had only been little more than half-a-year since he had stolen away on a hired pony. Now, he would ride down those same Mauchline streets next day on his own horse. He had gone from his family and friends to move among strangers in the hope of a second edition of his poems and here he was back, with new and important friends made, and the second edition in his pocket. Yes, it was a very different Robert Burns came back to Mauchline on the evening of Friday 8 June 1787.

Mauchline

Perhaps for the reason mentioned, he procrastinated even further by putting up at Johnny Dow's Tavern instead of going straight to Mossgiel. Or was it merely accidental that from the back window of the hostelry he could look across to Jean Armour's bedroom? One of the first things he did was to call on the Armours to see his two Jeans – mother and child. The other twin, as arranged, Robert, was with his mother and sisters at Mossgiel. His reception was not at all what he expected. And yet who can blame them? James Armour must have found it very difficult to reconcile this gentleman who now stood before him with the scapegrace, failed farmer who had left for Edinburgh. Like anyone who has tasted success, it showed in Burns's face and air. There was no denying he was now something, and the Armours dutifully bowed before it. Burns did not enjoy the situation as much as he thought he would. As he said later:

> If anything had been wanting to disgust me compleatly at Armour's family, their mean, servile compliance would have done it...

But, and this was significant, he added, 'I was made very welcome to visit my girl...'

Jean and he must have had a lot to talk about. If he had had his triumphs, she had had her travails. When her time had come with the twins, she had left the weaver in Paisley (A20) and come home to face the stigma and the rebuke of the Kirk Session. She agreed that the boy should go to Mossgiel and she would bring up the girl among the Armours. It was not an ideal situation but, in the circumstances, it was a practical one. However, it had applied when Burns, the recognised father of the children, had no prospects, but now...? James Armour couldn't believe his luck, but Jean knew her man better. She did not press him. She was content to wait.

Perhaps she remembered their first meeting at the Mauchline Race Week Dance just over three years before. She and Robert had been on the floor, when his dog, Luath, bounded in and jumped up between them, trying to claim the attention of his master, who merely called out – 'I wish I could find a lassie wad love me as much as my dug did!' Next afternoon, as Jean was laying out her mother's washing to dry on Mauchline Green, he and the dog passed, and he had to call Luath off, to stop him running over the clean sheets. Jean then reputedly called out (although she later denied it) – 'Weel, Mossgiel, have ye found your lass yet?' Looking at the shapely brunette she must have been at eighteen years of age, Burns must have known that he had. The timing, however, was not good. Burns could not very well openly pursue a courtship with one girl in the village while another in his house – Bess Paton – was awaiting his child, but that did not stop them expressing their love in the natural way. It seems that when James Armour was told by his wife that Jean was pregnant, he fainted. On being revived by the best cordial, he was then informed that Burns of Mossgiel was the father and fainted clean away again. The Armour family had then decided to take no more chances with the wilful Jean and packed her off to Paisley.

Mary Campbell had been a rebound affair from all of this, but it had still chilled him when he heard that she had died. He always felt somehow that he was to blame. He was never to lose his sense of guilt about her. Some said that she too was pregnant when she fell fatally ill from the fever but this has never been proved. Poor Burns couldn't pass a girl in a doorway without being accused of making her pregnant. Yet, in all the time he had been away – six months this time – he had had only one lapse and that was with May Cameron. Admittedly, it had not been for the want of trying with a few of the white-armed ladies met *en route*. Now, all that was past and here he was back with his 'delicious armful'.

> *When first I came to Stewart Kyle*
> *My mind it was nae steady*
> *Where e'er I gaed, where e'er I rade*
> *A mistress still I had ay;*
> *But when I came roun' by Mauchline toun,*
> *Not dreidin' any body*
> *My heart was caught before I thought*
> *And by a Mauchline lady.*

And she was never to let him go. Encouraged by her parents this time, she saw more of Burns than perhaps was good for both of them. It was hard to remember that in 1786 Armour had issued a warrant for Burns's arrest, and only the huge success of the Kilmarnock Edition had deflected its intent. Now Burns felt that Jean was being thrown at him. It was a precarious tactic and he retreated to Mossgiel to ponder matters. He was uneasy, because – 'the usual consequences began to betray her' – and altogether he was not too happy about his 'eclatant return to Mauchline'. As he wrote:

> The servility of my plebian brothers, who perhaps formerly eyed me askance, since I returned home, have nearly put me out of conceit altogether with my species.

He was glad to rejoin his family at Mossgiel, where he took to his bed claiming a fever. It was really just a chance to sort out his head. He wrote:

> I cannot settle to my mind. Farming is the only thing of which I know anything, and Heaven above knows, but little do I understand even of that. I cannot, I dare not, risk on farms as they are. If I do not fix, I will

go for Jamaica. Should I stay, in an unsettled state at home, I would only dissipate my little fortune and ruin what I intend shall compensate my little ones for the stigma I have brought upon their names.

For the first time in his life he was beginning to feel responsible, and he wasn't relishing it. The holiday was over and reality was looming on every side. Quite unusually for him, he was bored. To take his mind off it, he spent a lot of time writing a long autobiographical letter to a Dr John Moore in London:

To divert my spirits a little in this miserable fog of Ennui, I have taken a whim to give you a history of MYSELF...

This letter, begun on 2 August 1787, is the one that all the biographers and hagiographers have seized on ever since. Burns wrote a lot of letters from Mossgiel around this time. He wrote to Willie Nicol again telling him that he had bought himself a pocket Milton and had begun to study 'the magnaminity; the intrepid, unyielding independence, the desperate daring, the noble defiance of hardship in that great Personage – Satan.' Now he becomes introspective and worries about 'thoughtless follies and hare-brained whims, which, like some will o' the wisp, sparkle in the widely-gazing eyes of the poor, heedless Bard, till, POP, *he falls like Lucifer, never to hope again*'. The last phrase is not Milton, however, but Shakespeare – *Henry VIII*. The quotes from plays keep coming. A drama always seemed to be on the edge of his mind, but somehow it never comes to the fore. One remembers his original Tragic fragment from 1783. It too dealt with a devil. The idea had gone deep and never surfaced. He ends his letter – 'P.S. –I shall be in Edinr. about the latter end of July' – but in fact he did not make it till 7 August. Where did he go? The trail peters out around this time. It was as if Burns had gone to ground. It wasn't the first time he had taken off on his own. As a boy, to escape the drudgery of the farm, he 'stole out' to be on his own and think about his hero, William Wallace.

Syne to the Leglen wood, when it was late,
To beat a silent and a safe retreat...

I chose a fine summer Sunday, the only day my way of life allowed, and walked half a dozen of miles to pay my respect to the Leglen Wood with as much devout enthusiasm as ever pilgrim did to Loretto, and as I explored every den and dell where I supposed my heroic countryman to have lodged, I recollect – for even then I was a rhymer – my heart glowed with a wish to make a song on him...

That boy was still in the man. The song was to be written (*Scots Wha Hae*), but that was to come on another journey. Meantime, where was he?

Here am I – that is all I can tell you of that unaccountable being – myself.
What I am doing, no mortal can tell; what I am thinking, I myself cannot tell;
what I am usually saying is not worth saying.

Various Burns authorities have put their suggestions forward over the years. Raymond Lamont Brown, in his 1972 account of the tours, considers he may have gone to collect further book subscriptions, as the letter to Moore suggests. Snyder thinks he went to Greenock (A19) to expiate the memory of Mary Campbell. Catherine Carswell, in her fictionalised account, goes even further and says Burns sought out Mary's people in Dunoon. Dr James Mackay, more recently, puts forward a plausible theory that Burns rode from Glasgow (A10) to Greenock (A19), where he and his horse, Jenny Geddes, took the ferry to Dunoon so that he then was able to continue the horse-ride to Arrocher (A13). Mackay points out that this is, of course, pure conjecture, but it seems reasonable enough. Burns, on his own admission, was at that time in an agitated state, both mentally and emotionally. He might have done anything, but the last thing he wanted to do was make decisions. Hamlet-like, he drew out the limbo period as long as he could.

Since the Kilmarnock Edition which had come out nearly two years earlier, he had been talking, or been talked to, and perhaps now after the Borders tour, he was talked out. He needed time to get his breath back, and to me it makes great sense that he took time out and enjoyed his own company. It would also make sense to make a detour to Greenock from Glasgow, but then how often do we make sense when we have things on our mind? All we know for sure is that on 19 June he went from Mauchline (A7) to Kilmarnock (A8) and from there to Glasgow (A10).

Glasgow

Although it was the nearest big city to him, Burns paid less than a handful of visits to the metropolis on the Clyde. It was a busy, bustling place and Burns might have been attracted by its very energy, but it was a place he went to in order to get somewhere else, and in this case, it was to go into the West Highlands. He put up at the Black Bull Inn in Argyle Street, where a Marks and Spencer store now stands, and there met with Captain Richard Brown, his 'prompter' from Irvine (A6). They must have made a good night of it. 'One of the happiest occasions of my life', Burns later recalled. Further along Argyle Street lay the Trongate, on the north side of which Dr Moore, to whom Burns had so recently been writing, was born. The same Dr Moore was the grandson of a Glasgow Provost and the father of Sir John Moore of Corunna, and also a graduate of Glasgow University. Burns appeared to pay little attention to these Glasgow relevancies. Nor did he visit James Candlish – 'the earliest friend, except my own brother, that I have on earth' – who was then resident in the town. Instead, he called on John Smith, the Bookseller, and secured an order for 50 of his books from that same gentleman and wrote Creech accordingly. After that good morning's work, he pointed Jenny Geddes north by north west and rode out of the city in the company of a Glasgow man and fellow mason, Dr George Grierson, who had subscribed for no less than 36 copies of Burns's book. The good doctor was just the kind of friend every writer needs. Grierson kept a detailed record of his excursion with Burns but, unfortunately, it was lost in the Glasgow flood of 1831. However, some of his notes remain, and from these, and Burns's later letters, some idea of their itinerary can be deduced.

Inveraray

The two men are first picked up Tarbert (A11) *en route* to Inveraray (A12), the seat of John Campbell, the fifth Duke of Argyle. Why on earth Burns found himself here is impossible to answer. The Duke had indeed subscribed to the Edinburgh Edition, but that was a slim connection with which to seek hospitality of His Grace, although Burns did have Campbell blood in him on his father's side. As it turned out, the Duke was too busy hosting the British Fishery Society on the day they arrived and the inn was full of anglers. John Fraser, the innkeeper, not recognising the Bard, turned the travellers away. Angrily, Burns took his revenge by using his new diamond stylus on the nearest window pane:

Whoe'er he be that sojourns here,
I pity much his case.
Unless he comes to wait upon
The lord their God, 'His Grace'.
There's naething here but Highland pride,
And Highland scab and hunger,
If Providence ha sent me here,
'Twas surely in an anger.

One has the feeling that Burns was tired and hungry, and just angry enough himself to hold the stylus to the window. Needless to say, the pane was soon kicked out, but as happens in these cases, someone always takes a copy.

Appropriately, they returned by way of the pass aptly named Rest and be Thankful, continuing through Glen Croe to Crocharibus, by Arrochar (A13), on the heights overlooking Loch Long.

Arrochar

From Arrochar, he wrote to Ainslie:

I write you this on a tour through my country where savage streams tumble over savage mountains, thinly overspread with savage flocks, which starvingly support as savage inhabitants. My last stage was Inveraray (A12) – tomorrow night's stage, Dumbarton... (A18)

Sometime during the next day the two 'fell in with a merry party at a Highland gentleman's hospitable mansion'. This was Cameron House on the banks of Loch Lomond, where they danced 'till the ladies left us at three in the morning'. Burns described what happened afterwards in full detail in a letter to Jamie Smith.

...When the dear lasses left us, we ranged round the bowl till the good-fellow hour of six; except a few minutes when we went out to pay our devotions to the glorious lamp of day peering over the top of Benlomond. We all kneel'd: our worthy landlord's son held the bowl; each man a full glass in his hand; and I, as priest, repeated some rhyming nonsense, like Thomas a Rhymer's prophecies I suppose. – After a small refreshment of the gifts of Somnus, we proceeded to spend the day on Lochlomond, and reached Dumbarton in the evening. We dined at another good fellow's house, and consequently push'd the bottle; when we went out to mount our horses, we found ourselves 'No vera fou but gaylie yet'. My two friends and I rode soberly down the Loch side, till by came a Highlandman at the gallop, on a tolerably good horse, but which had never known the ornaments of iron or leather. We scorned to be out-galloped by a Highlandman, so off we started, whip and spur. My companions, though seemingly gayly mounted, fell sadly astern; but my old mare, Jenny Geddes, one of the Rosinante family, she strained past the Highlandman in spite of all his efforts, with the hair-halter: just as I was passing him, Donald wheeled his horse, as if to cross before me to mar my progress, when down came his horse, and threw his rider's breekless arse in a clipt hedge; and down came Jenny Geddes over all, and my bardship between her and the Highlandman's horse. Jenny Geddes trode over me with such cautious reverence, that matters were not so bad as might well have been

expected; so I came off with a few cuts and bruises, and a thorough resolution to be a pattern of sobriety for the future.

Next day, nursing their wounds – and their heads – they came
safely via Luss and Balloch (A17) to Dumbarton (A18).

Dumbarton

Here Burns was the guest of John McAuley, the Town Clerk, who
was no doubt instrumental in the granting of the Freedom of the
town to the poet, and the Burgess ticket dated 29 June 1787 testi-
fies to this. However, several Kirk voices in the district were raised
against honouring a man of such anti-clerical opinions. It is
strange that so many ministers today are recognised as expert
Burnsians, yet their predecessors in his own day were set against
him. It took time for Burns to be accepted by the cloth.

The following day he was seen by a Dr Taylor in Paisley (A20),
talking to a Mr Pattison in the street. Taylor recognised Burns
from the portrait in the book, and took the liberty of introducing
himself. He invited the poet to his house – and Mr Pattison came
too. They talked most of the afternoon away and the whole fam-

Paisley Abbey

ily, particularly the children, found
the famous author fascinating and
charming, although Mrs Taylor 'was
struck by certain gloominess that
seemed to have possession of his
countenance...' This little domestic
scene is one of the first instances of
Burns as a public figure away from
the mansions of the gentry and the
masons' lodges.

That 'certain gloominess' still hung about him on his return to
Mossgiel. From there, on 30 June, he wrote the letter quoted
above, about his race with the Highlander, to his old Mauchline
cronie, Jamie Smith, now in Linlithgow (D5). That letter goes on:

I have yet fixed on nothing with respect to the serious business of life.

> I am, just as usual, a rhyming, mason-making, raking, aimless, idle fel-
> low. However, I shall somewhere have a farm soon. I was going to say,
> a wife too: but that must never be my blessed lot...

This is such patent nonsense. Jean was at this time probably carrying their child – or children – although he was not to know this yet.

The last part of the letter goes on about his conquest of an un-named lady in an un-named place and has the air of callow *bravaccio* about it rather than the smell of truth. He was writing to an old familar, so he could write in this unbridled manner, but it doesn't sit right somehow. What is more credible is his comment in a letter to Ainslie a month later:

> I have not a friend on earth, beside yourself, to whom I can talk non-
> sense without forfeiting some degree of his esteem. Now, to one like
> me, who never cares for speaking anything but nonsense, such a friend
> as you is an invaluable treasure. I was never a rogue, but have been a
> fool all my life; and, in spite of all my endeavours, I see now plainly, that
> I shall never be wise...

Sometime at the beginning of August he sent his autobigraphical letter to Mrs Dunlop by the hand of her servant (who had come twenty miles to enquire about Burns's health on behalf of his mistress) before posting it off to Dr Moore in London. He told her in the accompanying note that he was leaving for Edinburgh 'the next day'. He did.

CHAPTER 5

The Highlands and the North East

(24 August to 23 September 1787)

Edinburgh – Corstorphine – Kirkliston – Winsburg – Boness – Linlithgow
– Falkirk – Bannockburn Stirling – Dunblane – Comrie – Arbruchill – Crieff
– Kenmore – Dunkeld – Inver – Aberfeldy – Killiecrankie – Blair Atholl
– Dalwhinnie – Pitmain (Kingussie) – Aviemore Dulsie – Kilravock
– Inverness – Nairn – Brodie – Forres – Elgin – Fochabers – Cullen – Banff
– Old Deer – Peterhead – Ellon – Old Aberdeen – Aberdeen – Stonehaven
– Montrose – Arbroath – Dundee – Perth – Kinross – Dunfermline
– Queensferry – Edinburgh.

*Tomorrow I leave Edinbr in a chaise. Nicol thinks it more
comfortable than horseback to which I say. Amen; so
Jenny Geddes goes home to Ayrshire to use a phrase of my
mother's – wi' her finger in her moo!*

It seems a shame that Jenny Geddes, his 'auld, jaud, glyde o' a
mere', who had carried him 'up hill and down brae in Scotland
and England as teuch and birnie as a very devil' should now be
dismissed 'wi' her finger in her moo', but Willie Nicol, his new
travelling companion who had Latin and Greek, had no equestri-
an skills. He insisted on a coach, as long as Burns shared the
expense. So it was agreed. Nicol
was also Burns's new landlord.
Sharing a coach was one thing, but
sharing a bed was another. Burns
moved out of John Richmond's single
room and took his farewell of the reli-
gious Mrs Carfrae and the not-so-reli-
gious neighbours upstairs. The Nicol family had an attic (B9) which they cleared for
the poet, but he was hardly unpacked
before he was off again. Although now

St Patrick Square

horseless, Burns was riding high in a sense. He still didn't have his feet on the ground. This was to be his last extravagance. Respectability loomed and he must prepare for it. Meantime, he would tour the Highlands in a coach with his irascible new landlord. Burns was later to describe Nicol's companionship as 'travelling with a loaded blunderbuss at full cock'. Only one person other than Burns is on record as actually liking Willie Nicol. This particular gentleman, Alexander Young ws, who met both men in Edinburgh, wrote of the schoolmaster:

> I considered him, and I believe justly, one of the greatest Latin scholars of the age; and when I found him & Burns over their Whiskey-punch, (which I sometimes had the honour of partaking with them) bandying extempore translations and imitations of English, Scotch and Latin epigrams, I could not help considering them as good exemplifications of the Italian improvisatori...at this time, I looked upon Nicol as a far greater poet than Burns...

It is to be hoped Mr Young had a change of mind, not that it mattered what a prissy Edinburgh solicitor thought. Burns liked his classical *compagnon de voyage* not only for his learning but also for his stamina at the drinking table. He hoped they would have ample opportunity to confirm this compatibility. There was more to share in the journey than the expenses. The experience would do them both good and get Burns out of Edinburgh for a time. That might do him more good than anything.

The further idea of the coach was that Burns would this time try to keep a journal of the journey with a view to future publication, but the result turned out to be much like the roads they travelled – fragmentary and disjointed. This trip, however, would allow him to meet up with his father's relatives in the North East, who, seemingly, had done much better than the south-west division of the family, some being lawyers and prosperous business men around Montrose. So it was with some

Kirkliston

curiosity that he 'set off for the North with the company of my good friend, Mr N'. He was heading north but he was also stepping back into history. This was an old Scotland he was going to see. Both were no doubt sitting back in some comfort as the chaise rolled through Corstorphine (D2) and out of Edinburgh to Kirkliston (D3) and Linlithgow (D5) ('what a poor, pimping business is a Presbyterian place of worship'), and on the Saturday to their first night stop at Falkirk (A43).

Falkirk

Crest on the front of the Carron Iron Works

Sunday 26 August – Carron Iron Works. One fails to see the tourist attraction of this place, but Burns had trouble here with petty authority which always riled him. The porter at the Iron Works gate would not let the visitors see round the place because it was a Sunday. Inevitably, the diamond stylus left its mark on the window of the Carron Inn:

We cam na here to view your works
In hopes to be mair wise
But only, lest we gang to hell,
It may be nae surprise...

'Came to Bannockburn'. This terse entry was all that the Field of Bannockburn (A44) inspired in him. 'Shown the old house where James 3rd was murdered – the hole where glorious Bruce sat up his standard – here no Scot can pass uninterested...come to Stirling'.

The site of Bruce's Standard

Stirling

Monday 27 August – Go to Harvieston – return in the evening to dine.

Burns shared with Nicol a common love for the old Royal House of the Stuarts. This awakened in Burns all his boyish patriotic fervour and caused him, after a good dinner no doubt, to write with his diamond pen some imprudent lines on the window of an inn at Stirling (A45) which were not all flattering to the reigning House of Hanover, calling them at one point:

An idiot race to honour lost,
Who know them best, despise them most.

He returned to the inn the next day meaning to kick out the offending pane but it was too late. Once again, as in Inveraray (A12), the lines had already been copied and were circulating fast.

The Golden Lion Hotel, Stirling

One has the feeling that everything Burns did on his tours was watched. He and Nicol hurried out of Stirling.

'Tuesday 28 August – cold reception at Arbruchill (D7) – sup at Crieff (D8).'

'Thursday 29 August – come down Tay to Dunkeld (D10) – pass Tay Bridge – Aberfeldy (D12).' Next day, they met with Niel Gow, the famous Scotch fiddler – 'a short, stout-built, honest, highland figure'. As a part-time fiddler himself, but virtually a full-time musicologist, Burns was delighted to be in the man's company in his own house. He and Gow talked old songs all day, and the older man was taken aback at the extent of Burns's musical knowledge, at least of the main body of Scots song. This was a growing part of Burns's creative concerns and he jumped at the chance of learning more. Nicol had to prise them apart in order to get under way again. It was not to be the last time that Nicol's haste and intemperate manners cut across his friend's desire to extend the pleasant hour and dally in good company. Burns surprisingly was mostly very patient with this aspect of Nicol's behaviour, although he may have had to restrain himself on most occasions. Then again, he was so often pressed to remain wherever he went, he might have stayed and never come back to Edinburgh at all. He loved what he called 'the social hour' but the trouble was it often extended into the whole night.

General Wade's Bridge, Aberfeldy

Blair Atholl

It was on now 'up the Tummel river to Blair'. At Blair Atholl (D14) he supped with the Duchess of Atholl. People were astonished at how at ease Burns was with gentlefolk, but then an extraordinary number of subscribers to both editions were of the higher class, from the Eglintons in Ayrshire to Glencairn and the gentlemen of the Caledonian Hunt in Edinburgh, not to mention the procession of titles met in the West Highlands. The truth was that he took his honesty with him wherever he went. This gave him a candour which was a welcome change among the welter of white lies, evasions and pretensions that made up so much social behaviour. He was a diversion and was welcomed for that as much as for his supposed celebrity. He scribbled verses and songs right and left as he went along and was happy to distribute them as requested. He may not have had to sing for his supper, but he certainly had to write for it. He did not mind. It was just like signing an autograph, and for him, just as easy. As he said,

Blair Castle, Blair Atholl

> Rhyme is the coin by which the poet pays his debts of honour and gratitude.

Without any doubt, for all his enjoyment of the ladies' attentions, the importance of the Blair Atholl visit over that weekend of 1-2 September was his meeting at the dinner-table with Robert Graham of Fintry. Graham was one of His Majesty's Commissioners of the Scottish Board of Excise, a connection that Burns was to bear very much in mind just a few years later. The Commissioner was captivated by the young poet's conversation and drawn also to his Jacobitism. The Duke and Duchess were similarly intrigued and asked him to stay on for a few days as Henry Dundas was expected. Whether Burns would have similarly appealed to the distinguished visitor is moot. Dundas, or 'King Henry' as he was called in Scotland, was officially Treasurer of the Navy but was indisputably the most powerful man in Scotland at that time, and a Tory. It is not known whether he was a lover of poetry, but it can be assumed he would have known of Burns. He knew everything that was happening in Scotland – that was his business. He might even have had Burns under surveillance. With Burns's firebrand reputation it was not beyond the bounds of possibility. At any rate, a meeting between them could have been more than useful to both sides but especially to a young man on the make, but Nicol was in his usual haste to continue, so Burns declined – again regretfully – and continued on his way.

According to Josiah Walker, the Duke's librarian, who was a strong admirer of Burns:

> The ladies, in their anxiety to have a little more of Burns's company, sent a servant to the inn, to bribe his driver to loosen or pull off a horse's shoe. But the ambush failed. Proh mirum. The driver was incorruptible.

However Burns or Nicol felt, the carriage rolled on.

> Sunday 2 September – Come up the Garrie – Falls of Bruar.
> Monday 3 September – breakfast at Aviemore (D17) – through mist and darkness to Dulsie (D18) to lie.

No mention of the fact that they had to find their way through

Cawdor Castle

seventeen feet of snow before entering Strathspey and making it into Aviemore.

Tuesday 4 September – came down the Findhorn to Cawdor – 'saw the bed on which King Duncan was stabbed' – dined at Kilravock (D19) with the Rose family.

Burns was immediately taken with the warm welcome they gave him.

There was something in my reception at Kilravock so different from the cold, obsequious, dancing-school bow of politeness, that it almost got into my head that friendship had occupied her ground without the intermediate march of acquaintance.

Again one is struck by Burns's striking and pertinent prose. Once more there was another reluctant farewell before they moved on to Fort George and Inverness (D20).

Inverness

At Kingsmills House, Nicol noticed that Burns was 'thoughtful and silent during the evening'. Burns described himself as 'jaded with the fatigue of today's journey'. Once again he was feeling the strain of being 'on show'. Nicol could stump ahead of the company or trail moodily behind, but Burns had always to be there in the spotlight. Where two or more were gathered together, he had to be in the centre of them.

The Culloden Monument

Thursday 6 September – Come over Culloden Moor – reflections on the field of battle – dine at Nairn (D21) – to Brodie House (D22) to lie. Friday 7 September – Mr Brodie tells me the muir where Shakespeare lays Macbeth's witch meeting is still haunted – cross the Findhorn to Forres (D23) – breakfast at Elgin (D24) – cross the Spey to Fochabers (D25).

Fochabers

Here, an invitation came to dine at Castle Gordon with the Duke and Duchess, but it was for Burns alone and not for Nicol. Dr Robert Couper, a fellow-guest, remembers what happened:

> At the castle, our poet was received with the utmost hospitality and kindness...He was invited to take his place at the table as a matter of course...but after a few glasses of wine, he rose up and proposed to withdraw. On being pressed to stay, he mentioned, for the first time, his engagement with his fellow traveller; and his noble host, offering to send a servant to conduct Mr Nicol to the table, Burns insisted on undertaking that office himself...but it was too late. Nicol had ordered the horses to be put into the carriage, being determined to proceed on the journey alone...Parading before the entrance to the inn, he was venting his anger on the postillion for his slowness...No explanation or entreaty would make him change his mind...Our poet was reduced to the necessity of separating from him entirely or of instantly proceeding...He chose the latter...and seating himself in the post-chaise, with mortification and regret turned his back on Gordon Castle.

It must have seemed a long way for both of them to the next stage at Cullen (D26). Burns had no compunction about putting the blame squarely on Nicol. In his 'Thank You' poem to the Gordon's librarian, James Hoy, he spoke of:

> That unlucky predicament which hurried me, tore me away from Castle Gordon. May that obstinate son of Latin prose be curst to Scotch-mile periods, and damned to seven-league paragraphs; while Declension & Conjugation, Gender, Number and Time, under the ragged banners of Dissonance and Disarrangement eternally rank against him in hostile array!!!!!!

Six exclamation marks would indicate his desire for effect, but there was a good head of steam beneath it all the same. Nicol and he were good friends but not perhaps ideal travelling companions. They were both under different strains. The literary lion had been paired with the academic bear and both were beset by social jackals. Each reacted in his own way to these stresses, and it can be assumed that the atmosphere inside the post-chaise must have been warm at times. So, having missed out on Henry Dundas at Blair, Burns now missed the chance of an improving acquaintance with the Duchess of Gordon. His luck was not in, at least in terms of social advancement. Who knows what might have transpired had he met Dundas, and the same applies to a further acquaintance with the influential Jane Gordon who was more than happy to meet him halfway. But it was not to be.

Their driver now cracked the whip over the horses, heading them towards Banff (D27). Nicol was still in the huff and spent all the time they were at Duff House huddled in the library. George Imlach, then a boy at the local Academy, was their guide while in the town. When asked if he knew who Burns was, he replied, 'Oh, aye. We hae his book at hame'. He was then asked to name his favourite Burns poem, and he replied at once, *'The Twa Dugs* and *Death and Doctor Hornbook* although I like *The Cotter's Saturday Night* best because it made me greet when my faither read it tae my mither.' At this, Burns, who hadn't spoken, placed his hand on the boy's shoulder, saying – 'Weel, my callant, I don't wonder at your greetin'...It made me greet mair than aince when I wis writin' it.' It is charming to think of the poet's enjoying a moment like this with a clever young schoolboy who was never to forget it. Years later he said, 'The face and look of Robert Burns were such as man or boy could not forget.' On that Saturday (8 September) Burns and Nicol enjoyed 'a pleasant ride along the shore. Country almost as wild again between Banff and Newbyth – quite wild as we came thro' Buchan to Old Dear'. Burns, no doubt, meant Old Deer, which they left next morning for Peterhead and brought them back to the coast road again at the Bullers of Buchan. Dined at Ellon – passing Ellon House, home of Geordie Gordon, the bad Earl, who forbade all visitors because of the young mistress he housed there. As Burns put it – Entrance denied to everybody owing to the jealously of three-score over a kept country wench. They came into New Aberdeen by way of Old Aberdeen and they lodged at the New Inn in Castle Street.

Aberdeen

At the Granite City (D32), among a whole roomful of local nota-
bles, Burns met with Professor Thomas Gordon ('a good-natured,
jolly-looking Professor of Philosophy') and Bishop John Skinner,
son of the author of *Tullochgorum* which Burns described as 'The
best Scotch Song Scotland ever saw'. Burns spent more than an
hour most agreeably with the Bishop, despite Nicol's hurrying him
once again, and in that time Burns said, 'We had fifty auld sangs
through our hands'. He also learned from the cleric that their carriage had passed only four miles from the home of the senior
Skinner. Burns replied, 'Never did a devotee of the Virgin Mary go
to Loretto with more fervour than I would have approached his
dwelling and worshipped at his shrine.' This was not only a clever
allusion to the Bishop's calling as well as a tribute to his father, it
also echoed a similar outburst from Burns on visiting Leglen
Woods as a boy. Like all great writers, Burns was never one to
waste a good metaphor. Similarly, he had favourite phrases and
turns of speech and they recur in his letters from time to time.
Bishop Skinner wrote of Burns to his father:

> As to his general appearance, it is very much in his favour. He is a
> genteel-looking young man of good address, and talks with as much
> propriety as if he had received an academical education. He has indeed
> a flow of language, and seems never at a loss to express himself in the
> strongest and most nervous manner...

Burns had asked the Bishop for his father's address, explaining
'Perhaps he might assist me in the collection of auld sangs I am
making on these journeys?' Skinner's address was given him. We
can see now that Burns had abandoned the idea of a publishable
journey in favour of a collection of old Scots songs. Posterity was
to be grateful for this change of mind.

Montrose

My ancient, but ignoble blood
Has crept through scoundrels since the Flood...

It was now time to seek out his father's family. He made contact
with his cousin, James Burness, in Stonehaven (D33), and wrote to
his brother Gilbert at Mossgiel:

I spent two days among our relations, and found our aunts, Jean and
Isobel, still alive and hale old women. John Caird, though born the same
year as our father, walks as vigorously as I can...William Brand is likewise a stout old fellow...

Burns had always had a fascination about his forebears. He
knew the story of his father's family at Clochnahill, near Dunottar,
being broken up at the time of the '45 Jacobite rebellion, and
about the brothers scattering throughout Scotland. His father's
brother James went to Montrose (D34) and founded the dynasty
of lawyers. It was a son of this family who first petitioned the Lord
Lyon for a family coat of arms in 1837. It took until 1988 for this
to be granted. Ironically, the design that was finally accepted was
virtually that which Burns himself was to suggest in a letter to
Cunningham in March 1794:

On a field azure, a holly bush, seeded proper; in base, a shepherd's pipe
and crook, saltier-wise, also in proper, in chief. On a wreath of the
colours, a woodlark perching on a sprig of bay tree, proper. For crests,
two mottoes: Round the top of the crests – 'Woodnotes Wild'. At the
bottom of the shield, in the usual place – 'Better a wee bush than nae
bield'...

For a man ostensibly in fun, his description was remarkably
detailed and one can only admire his grasp of heraldic language.
'Secundem artem, my Arms!' he had said half in earnest, but perhaps, at heart, he meant to be taken seriously. There was a good
part of the snob in Robert Burns, and he dearly would have loved
to have been a lord, despite all his egalitarian protestations,
although there is no denying their sincerity. Something always nig-
gled him about the unlucky station into which he had been born.

Because of the suggestion that through the name Burness or Burnes there was an Argyle connection with the Campbells, the original application for matriculation of arms did include the Campbell insignia, but this was removed in further applications. The coat of arms was eventually approved in Burns's original design and can now be seen in association with the Burns Federation. Burns may have been the first to want it, but it was the continued efforts of the Burness clan in Montrose that finally got the family crest, even if it took them 194 years to do it.

Meantime, on Tuesday 11 September – 'Meet with Mr Burnes – lie at Laurencekirk'. He describes his lawyer cousin as 'one of those who love fun, a gill, a punning joke and have not a bad heart'. At Lawrencekirk they met with 'a jolly, frank, sensible, love-inspiring widow', but Burns does not mention her name. Once again, he wanted to stay longer with his hospitable relatives. One can imagine how, among them, thoughts of his father must have come back to him, but Nicol was chivvying him to move on as usual. The Latin master was becoming homesick as they turned the post-chaise towards Arbroath (D35) and the road south. In actual fact, they went by boat to reach this seaside town - the first time Burns had ever been out to sea in a ship and he hardly mentioned it – other than 'land, dine at Arbroath'.

Their chaise took them on to Dundee (D36), but still Nicol hurried them despite 'his Bardship's being almost in love with Miss Bess Scott at breakfast'.

They went on through the Carse of Gowrie to Perth (D37). On 15 September they rode out to see Scone Palace, but

Village Cross, Scone

Burns was too ill to take it in and tersely recorded, 'Came to Kinross (D38) to lie – reflections in a fit of colic'.

The Highland tour ended next day with a further laconic entry:

Pass through a cold, barren country to Queensferry (D42) – dine – cross the ferry and on to Edinbr...

Their Highland excursion had lasted 22 days and covered almost 600 miles ('windings included') and, what is almost as astonishing, his friendship with Willie Nicol had survived it, despite all the latter's impatience and self-ishness. Burns seemed to understand him. Josiah Walker perhaps explains this best in his report of a conversation he had at Blair with Burns as he walked him to his carriage. He quoted a remark the poet had made about Nicol who was walking a few paces before them. Walker said:

Lantern Tower,
North Queensferry

> (Nicol) was a man of robust, but clumsy person; and while Burns was expressing to me the value he entertained for him, on account of his vigorous talents, although they were clouded at times by his coarseness of manners; 'In short', he added, 'his mind is like his body, he has a confounded, strong, in-kneed sort of a soul.

It takes one good man to see another.

He gave another view of the tour to Patrick Miller at Dalswinton (A24): 'My journey through the Highlands was perfectly inspiring; and I hope to have laid in a good stock of poetical ideas from it...' In a postscript he added, 'I am determined not to leave Edinburgh until I wind up matters with Mr Creech, which I am afraid will be a tedious business...' It was.

He was asked to wait while Creech dealt with the accounts to hand. Burns waited two weeks and then, in case he took a cudgel to the publisher, and perhaps keen to get out of Nicol's attic, he decided on another short tour, this time on horseback. He had had a long-standing invitation to visit Sir William Murray at Ochtertyre (D40) as well as from other gentlemen in the vicinity, but perhaps the real reason for the tour was the chance of renewing acquaintance with Miss Peggy Chalmers who, like Burns, was to be a guest at Harvieston House for the week. Burns had met her first in Edinburgh during the previous winter when she had played the piano for the blind Dr Blacklock. Burns called her 'Dear Countrywoman' because her father had a farm near Mauchline

(A7). If she wasn't gentry, she was certainly genteel. Her mother was a sister of Gavin Hamilton, Burns's lawyer. Burns had written two songs about her and this was reason enough to pursue her into Stirlingshire.

A Tour of Stirlingshire

This was to be Burns's fourth trip in the year. This time he rode out in the company of young Dr Adair, a kinsman of Mrs Dunlop, who kept the account of their excursion.

4 October 1787 – Left Edinburgh by Linlithgow (D5) and Carron to Stirling.

Linlithgow Palace and Loch

It is hard to believe Burns would have bothered about the Iron Works again. Adair may be mistaken here. At Stirling (A45) they met with a group of travellers from Edinburgh which included Nicol. This seems odd as well. However, Adair does report that 'Their conversational sparks delighted the company' – so we'll take his word for it.

Next morning, they rode into Clackmannanshire by the Vale of Devon to Harvieston (A49). Adair was to meet his future wife, the eldest daughter of Mrs Hamilton, here. He was always to be grateful to Burns for inviting him to join the party at Harvieston, for the marriage proved to be very happy. Burns actually stayed eight days at the house, plus two 'storm-steaded at the foot of the Ochils' due to bad weather.

That week at Harvieston was arguably one of the happiest of his life. Not since the creative years at Lochlie was he so at one with himself and content with life as he was in the congenial company of those present – Sir William Murray, John Ramsay, Mrs Hamilton, and of course, Peggy Chalmers. She made him more than welcome and he joined in the events of the week with zest. They saw Castle Campbell, the Caldron-linn and the Rumbling Bridge, among other local sights. For once he wasn't on show. He felt he was among friends. So idyllic was the occasion that he took the opportunity, despite the long shadow of Jean Armour on his back, to propose marriage to Peggy. It says much for Miss Chalmers that she refused him without losing his affection or friendship. One can only surmise the effect such a union might have had on his future life. Exactly a year later, when he was married to Jean and installed at Ellisland, he wrote to Peggy Chalmers:

> When I think I have met with you, and have lived more of real life with you in eight days than I can do with almost anybody I have met with in eight years – when I think on the improbability of meeting you in this world again – I could sit down and cry like a child!

Peggy married Lewis Hay, an Edinburgh banker, in 1788 but she remained for Burns 'in his heart's core as a female friend', until she died a widow in Pau, near Berne in Switzerland, in 1843. She never forgot she had been proposed to by Robert Burns. She was one of the three women of quality (Nancy McLehose and Maria Riddell were the others) that Burns was to admire, and who knows, she might have made Burns a wonderful wife.

Meantime, apparently unscathed by his marriage rejection, Burns went off with Adair to visit Mrs Bruce of Clackmannan (A47), who was then over 90 years of age but still a vigorous and vociferous descendant of the Scottish royal line. She had the custody of Bruce's helmet and two-handed sword, which she used, there and then, to confer a knighthood on Burns, saying she had more right to do so *'than some people'*. Adair goes on:

Dunfermline Abbey, the Refectory

> At Dunfermline (D41) we visited the ruined Abbey, and the Abbey church, now consecrated to Presbyterian worship. Here, I mounted the cutty stool, or stool of repentance, assuming the character of a penitent for fornication; while Burns from the pulpit addressed to me a ludicrous reproof and exhortation, parodied from that which had delivered to himself in Ayrshire when he had mounted the seat of shame.

Adair might admire Burns's gift as an actor, but Ramsay of Ochtertyre (D39), their host and himself a classical scholar of some repute, was adamant about the possibilities of Burns as a dramatist. He left a short memorandum of Burns's visit to him:

I have been in the company of many men of genius, some of them poets, but never witnessed such flashes of intellectual brightness as from him. In the impulse of the moment, sparks of celestial fire! I was never more delighted therefore than with his company for two days, tete-a-tete. In mixed company, I should have made little of him, for, in the gamester's phrase, he did not always know when to play off and when to play on...I not only proposed to him the writing of a play similar to 'The Gentle Shepherd', qualem dicet esse sororem but Scottish Georgics, a subject which Thomson has by no means exhausted in his Seasons. What beautiful landscapes of rural life and manners might not have been expected from a pencil so faithful and forcible as his...

Burns showed no interest however, and the chance was passed. Pity. It was the nearest he had come to writing a play. According to his first biographer, Currie, Burns did decide on the title of a play – Rob McQuechan's Elshon – the plot of which concerned one McQuechan, Bruce's cobbler, who accidentally drove an awl into the royal foot, but Dr David Daiches, the noted Burns scholar, who has always insisted that there was a great deal of the play-actor in Burns, is less certain there was a dramatist. Ramsay, however, persisted in this attempt to interest Burns in writing a pastoral play, but there is no record of the poet's ever putting a pen to paper to write a play. Perhaps it was just that he was not in the right frame of mind. As he wrote to Nicol, 'I find myself very comfortable here, neither oppressed by ceremony nor mortified by neglect'. He could not, however, remain a country guest forever. He must get back to real life and prise some cash out of Creech.

On 20 October, after some delay at Alva (A48), he and Adair were rowed across the Forth at Queensferry and returned to Edinburgh.

CHAPTER 6

Edinburgh Re-Visited

I have both a second and a third edition going on...

THE FIRST THING HE DID on returning to the Capital was to catch a cold which laid him low again. Sensing that he might be in Edinburgh longer than he thought, the second thing he did was to change his 'digs'. He moved from one attic to another. William Cruickshank was the Rector of the High School and, like Burns, one of Nicol's few friends. Now he offered Burns the top floor of the Cruikshank house at No 2 St James Square (B10) at the east end of Princes Street as his Edinburgh accommodation. Despite being confined to his bed, Burns was delighted with his new lodgings. Ainslie lived in the same square as did another law student, Alexander Cunningham, who was to prove a good friend. Burns soon enjoyed walks over Arthur's Seat with his friends and sober 'tea-drinkings' instead of the usual bottle each.

St. James's Square

It made a welcome change. Ainslie said he had never known Burns so amusing and delightful as he was while they strolled over the hill and through the streets.

Then a letter came (probably from Gilbert) to tell Burns that his two-year-old daughter Jean had died suddenly at the Armour house in Mauchline (A7). She had died on the very day that Burns was being rowed across the Forth at Queensferry with Dr Adair. He mentioned his loss to John Richmond, who had returned to Mauchline during the Edinburgh recess –

> By the way, I hear I am a girl out of pocket and by careless, murdering mischance too, which has provoked me and vexed me a great deal...

No doubt. The 'by the way' hides the frustration and anger he

79

must have felt at what he suspected was lack of care by the Armours, but he made no attempt to return to Mauchline. He took a quick trip to Dumfries (A23) 'to wait on Mr Miller about his farms' but could not trust himself to face the Armours again. As for Jean, she must cope as best as she could in the meantime. There was nothing he could do for her. So he returned to his Edinburgh pursuits. There is a poignant irony in the fact that the first thing he did was to write a song for the daughter of the house where he now lodged. The twelve-year-old Jenny Cruikshank, whom Burns called 'Rosebud', was learning to play the harpsichord, and Burns had promised her that if she practised, he would write a song especially for her. Josiah Walker provides a nice picture of both when he arranged to meet Burns in Edinburgh:

> About the end of October, I called for him at the house of a friend, whose daughter, though not more than twelve, was a considerable proficient in music. I found him seated at the harpsichord of this young lady, listening with the keenest interest to his own verse, which she sung and accompanied, and by adjusting them to the music by repeated trials of the effect. In this occupation he was totally absorbed, that it was difficult to draw his attention from it for a moment.

It is not the first instance of his easy relationship with children and young people. The result of their absorption was the very popular *A Rosebud By My Early Walk*.

He was to remain 'totally absorbed' in Scots song from this point on. More and more in the recent Highland tour he had given himself over to consideration of song rather than any poetic fancy. In fact, none of the tours produced anything of high merit in either line, although from the time of his various encounters *en route* – with Gow, with the pretty singing of assorted misses throughout, with Skinner's son in Aberdeen and even with Ramsay at Ochtertyre, his mind was pointed more and more towards song.

This month of November 1787 was the first chance he had to give to Johnson's scheme to collect and print a *Scottish Musical Museum* since meeting with the worthy engraver at the Crochallen Fencibles the year before. Burns had known at once that it was a project exactly after his own heart. No one in Scotland was more fitted, both in terms of lyric skill and musical knowledge, to carry the thing through. Johnson could not afford to pay for his services, but Burns only shrugged the matter off. He explained the position more fully to James Hoy, when he wrote to the latter asking for a copy of *Cauld Kail in Aberdeen* –

> An engraver, James Johnson, in Edinburgh, has, not from mercenary views, but from an honest Scotch enthusiasm, set about collecting all our native songs and setting them to music; particularly those that have never been set before. Clarke, the well-know musician, presides over the musical arrangements; and Drs Beattie & Blacklock, Mr Tytler, Mr Woodhouselee, and your humble servant to the utmost of his small power, assist in collecting the old poetry, or sometimes, for a fine air to make a stanza when it has no words...I look on it as no small merit to this work that the names of many of the authors of our old Scotch Songs, names almost forgotten, will be remembered.

Little did he realise that by his work on this, and by a succeeding scheme to be set up by George Thomson, his own name would be enhanced as much as it had been by his poetry. Indeed, there are many who consider Robert Burns a greater lyricist than lyric poet, but to him I am sure they were one and the same thing. To catch the moment of feeling and interpret the truth of it a line so that it lives forever, that was always his hope, and whether in a poem or a song would matter little. There was no doubt, however, that he was becoming increasingly biased towards songs. They were more and more his priority and before long, he was virtually sole editor of the whole project. Ideally, had such an editorship been possible professionally for him at this time, it would have saved his worrying about farming or bothering about the Excise, and, not to put too fine a point on it, might have saved his life – or at least, delayed his death.

He had all the right qualities for the job – an ear for a good tune, an eye for the essentials of lyric, and the taste to put them together effectively. There was no archness or artificial insipidity so evident in songs of that time, especially when he worked on the fragments. These ancient songs came out of the very earth of Scotland. They were thick with tradition and tempered by the voices of generations who had passed them on. There was no need for Burns to pose, or strike any attitude, he merely had to collate the best of them. In this way the *Museum* would house a whole body of Scots song that otherwise might have been lost. John Ramsay, who had hoped for the playwright in Burns, had also spotted the song-writer. After Burns had returned from Stirlingshire to Edinburgh, Ramsay sent him another friendly injunction:

> Let those bright talents that the Almighty has bestowed on you, be henceforth employed to the noble purpose of Truth and Virtue. An imagination so varied and forcible as yours may do this in many different modes; nor is it necessary to be always serious, which you have been to good purpose; good morals may be recommended in a comedy – or even a song.

Burns had all the enthusiasm and energy vital to such a plan. When any of his partners were lax, or late in their contributions, he was on to them at once. For instance, he was constantly chasing Stephen Clarke:

> Mr B is deeply impressed with, & awefully conscious of, the high importance of Mr C's time, whether in the winged moments of symphonious exhibition at the keys of Harmony, while listening seraphs ease their own delightful strains; or, in the drowsy hours of slumbrous repose, in the arms of his dearly-beloved elbow-chair, where the frowsy, but potent power of Indolence, circumfuses her vapours round, & sheds her dews on the beard of her darling son - but half a line conveying half a meaning from Mr C would make Mr B the very happiest of mortals.

Mr Clarke replied. And when Johnson, the initiator of the enterprise, became dispirited and pessimistic, Burns was quick to reassure him:

> You are a Patriot for the Music of your Country; and I am certain Posterity will look on themselves as highly indebted to your Publick spirit...Your Work is a great one...To future ages your Publication will be text-book & standard of Scottish Song and Music.

Peggy Chalmers demurred about one of his songs written for her, *My Peggy's Charms*, being included in the Museum –

I love my Peggy's angel air,
Her face so truly heavenly fair,
Her native grace so void of art;
But I adore my Peggy's heart.

She said she was embarrassed and wanted him to withdraw
the song but Burns was quick to answer her:

The compliments I pay cannot be misunderstood. They are neither of
them so particular as to point you out to the world at large; and the
circle of your acquaintance will allow all that I have said. Besides, I have
complimented you chiefly, almost solely, on your mental charms. Shall
I be plain with you? I will; so look to it. Personal attractions, madam, you
have much above par; wit, understanding and worth, you possess in the
first class. This is a cursed, flat way of telling you these truths, but let
me hear no more of your sheepish timidity.

The reply shows all Burns's confidence with words, especially
when allied to a strong idea. This was the basis of his lyric skill,
and his touch, for the most part, was unerring as a *belletrist*. He
was to have further proof of this in his next Edinburgh episode.
Yet during all this song-time, even if he was, in his own words,
'hurried, puzzled, plagued and confounded with some disagreeable matters', the best of him went into this musical collection.
The 'disagreeable matters' were his on-going disputes with Creech
about his money and with the Armours about Jean, her own doubtful condition and the effects of little Jean's death on both of them,
the continued correspondence with Patrick Miller about terms and
conditions in a lease of Ellisland, and with Graham of Fintry and
others about a commission in the Excise. He could not make up his
mind on whether to be a farmer or an exciseman, and to his lasting
regret, he was to try to play both parts. However, it was time again
to don the social motley, but already he could feel the tide of his
novelty receding. The Ploughman Poet had had his hour.

Had it not been for Creech's procrastination, he would already
have been gone from the city, but he was forced to stay on. It was
not that Creech denied Burns's claims, it was only that he was
reluctant to part with cash at all. It was his normal method not to
pay until he had to, and Burns just had to keep knocking at his

door. He knew he would get the full amount – eventually. What he did not bank on, however, was meeting someone who would change his whole attitude to Edinburgh and to other aspects of his complicated private life. Like everything that happened to him, it seemed to do so all at once, and with the usual life-changing consequences. Robert Burns never did anything by halves, and this next involvement was to be no exception.

Agnes McLehose was a Glasgow girl, petite and blonde – 'and with features that were regular and pleasing... A well-formed mouth displayed teeth beautifully white'. Daughter of a surgeon, Andrew Craig, and niece of a Presbyterian minister, she was also cousin and second cousin to two Edinburgh judges, so it can be seen that '*pretty Nancy Craig*' was well connected. She was also impulsive. At eighteen she had run away to Edinburgh with a writer from Glasgow, James McLehose, and four sons later, *he* had run away from *her* to the West Indies, leaving her and her boys to the charity of relatives and friends. This then was the 'grass-widow' Burns met at a tea party given by Miss Erskine Nimmo at her brother's flat on the north side of Alison Square (B11) on 4 December 1787.

> *When dear Clarinda, matchless fair,*
> *First struck Sylvander's raptur'd view,*
> *He gaz'd, he listen'd to despair –*
> *Alas! 'twas all he dared to do!*

Burns had no chance of not falling in love – and he knew what love was, if anyone did – 'Love is the Alpha and the Omega of human enjoyment...it is the spark of celestial fire that lights up wintry hut of poverty and makes the cheerless mansion warm...' Being in love was a necessary condition with him. Not for the sex it naturally posited, but for the sheer happiness of the feeling itself. I am convinced this was the source of his creativity in poetry. He *loved* everything he wrote about – from mice to men, from sheep to woodlarks, but above all, he loved women. And Nancy McLehose was easy to fall in love with. She was everything he liked in a female – witty, intelligent, well-read, vivacious – and blonde. 'Golden locks are a sign of amorousness' he had once written. One has only to remember Mary Campbell, May Cameron, Jean Lorimer, Jean Jaffrey and Anna Park as other blondes in his life. Unlike these girls, however, Nancy McLehose was educated, and even had pretensions to being a poet herself. She was also brave. Despite her straitened circumstances, she held her place in Edinburgh society. She kept her sons on ten shillings a week and on the impact her abandonment had made on that same society. She depended on their charity for her living and her good name. She had to be careful, but was determined to meet Burns. When they did meet, it took both of them by surprise. Their attraction was mutual and immediate.

Before leaving Miss Nimmo's soirée, they made arrangements to meet at Nancy McLehose's house for tea on the following Saturday, and it would seem that neither could wait for the time to come. Burns, meantime, had forced a hundred pounds out of Creech and was celebrating on the Friday at the theatre with his actor friend, William Woods, and other theatricals. Burns was in a coach with Woods when it overturned at a corner. Both Burns and Woods blamed the driver for being drunk, but neither, it may be gathered, was in a position to make a sober judgement. The upshot was that Burns dislocated his kneecap and was forced to rest in his rooms with the injured leg on a chair. Naturally he had to cancel his appointment for the Saturday night and sent an urgent note to Nancy –

> I can say with truth, Madam, I never met a person I was more anxious
> to meet again, but an unlucky fall from a coach...

She replied immediately with a murmur of sympathy but with a hint of what he referred to as '*some unnamed feeling, stronger than a whim...*' He caught the scent immediately. This was exactly his kind of sport and he sent the porter back again with another letter – 'I fear I go wrong in my usual, unguarded way...' He knew exactly what he was doing. So did she. 'If I was your sister, I should call and see you; but 'tis a censorious world this; and, in this sense, you and I are not of this world...'

Yes, they were well matched. It was a love game in every sense. In no time, they had both whipped themselves into a paper passion

– without either stirring from their respective rooms. At one point, they were writing six letters a day to each other. The pace was getting too much for Burns. As an antidote he took to reading the Bible from start to finish, but he could not stop himself writing that he was 'ready to hang himself for love of her'. Putting the actual word on paper was too much for Nancy, but Burns would not be deflected:

> You say we cannot talk of love – then put 'respect', 'esteem', or any other tame, Dutch expression you like in its place...

It was then that Nancy showed her poise. She suggested that perhaps they should each use a *nom de plume* – adopt Arcadian names 'Clarinda' and 'Sylvander' in keeping with the letter of the correspondence, if not the underlying spirit. It was a strategy that would allow them at least a modest cover. As she said, 'I feel somewhat less restraint when I sign myself Clarinda...' I am sure she did. One can only wonder what might have been said between them had they had recourse to a telephone. The name-game made little difference to Burns. 'I like the idea of Arcadian names in commerce of this kind.'

He had not only found another character to play, he had been given a name for it. Behind its mask, he could now say more or less what he liked, and he said it well, for in the role of the professed lover he was ideally cast. After all, he had played the role from the time he was Mauchline's memorable blackfoot speaking and writing on behalf of his country compears in their love affairs in the manner of a latter-day Cyrano de Bergerac. Now he could put that early writing practice to good use. There seemed little point in any discretion however. To send so many letters by Williamson's Penny Post was not the most anonymous way to correspond. Nancy sent hers by way of her maid, Jenny Clow. Sometimes, young Jenny had to wait in Burns's room while he wrote his reply to Clarinda. This posed its own problem, as Jenny was to find out nine months later. The trouble was that Burns was beginning to believe his own script. He was now in a hurry to get to the denouement. On 4 January 1788, he wrote:

> Tomorrow evening I intend taking a chair and paying a visit at Park

> Place to a much-valued old friend. If I could be sure of finding you at home, I will send one of the chairmen to call. I would spend from five to six o'clock with you as I go past. I cannot do more at this time...

Such writing was as much part of his nature as of his talent. He had trained himself for it since his first letters in 1781. His style is assured because he knows he is winning.

> Don't think I flatter you or have designs upon you...I may take a fort by storm but never by siege...Do we not sometimes exchange faults rather than get rid of them...He who sees you as I have done and does not love you, deserves to be damned for his stupidity. He who loves you and would injure you, deserves to be doubly damned for his villainy...I love to madness and I feel to torture...I am yours, Clarinda, for life...

One can almost hear the points being scored. Nancy would have to have been very hard-hearted indeed to resist the full avalanche of words that descended on her, and it is words that win most women. Yet she kept her head, if not her heart. She wrote quickly to Burns, asking him not to come by chair but on foot, saying – 'A chair is so uncommon a thing in our neighbourhood, it is apt to cause speculation'. However much she was infatuated, or even genuinely in love, she was still a well-brought-up Edinburgh matron; but being at heart the more adventurous Glasgow girl, she was less worried about his departure – 'The neighbours are all asleep by ten'.

Nancy met him flanked by her relations, the Reverend Craig and William Craig, the lawyer. The night was saved for decorum and the neighbours. Burns vented his frustration on the ever-willing Jenny Clow. She didn't need to be wooed by letter. She couldn't read. Nancy was in control again, but it had been a very close thing.

> I will not deny it, Sylvander, last night was one of the most exquisite that I have experienced. Few such fall to the lot of mortals!...Today's reflections have not been altogether mixed with regret...no more. The opinion Sylvander may have formed from my unreservedness; and, above all, some secret misgivings that Heaven may not approve, situated as I am. These procured me a sleepless night.

Burns love-tactic in always aiming for intimacy at once did not seem to work with gentlewomen. It was not that he was brutish, but rather that his methods accorded to his station. He realized that he was being kept at a distance in all his tender dealings with the fair sex at any higher level, even when, as with Clarinda, and Peggy Chalmers, and later, Maria Riddell, a measure of his own feeling was returned.

That it was by Nancy McLehose is shown by her having her silhouette done by Miers, who had already done Burns in outline. She presented it to Burns as a breast-pin. (He was to wear it at all times, and it was buried with him.) Such an overt act was reckless, and the couple were now being talked about. Nancy tried to draw back and wrote to Burns asking him not to see her again, but he dismissed her letter as 'Puritanic scrawl and Damned sophistry' and rightly suspected the work of her guardian behind it. He was beginning to get really fed up with Edinburgh society – 'bucks strutting, ladies flaring, blackguards sculking, whores leering &c, in the old way' – and he 'still hadn't got the better of my bruised knee, but I have laid aside my crutches – a lame poet is unlucky; lame verses is an everyday circumstance...' He had sold himself as an unlettered ploughboy and now he couldn't shake off the tag. The social stigma stuck and it inhibited any move to strike outwards and upwards. He was intelligent enough to see how the world worked and now that he had been rebuffed for the second time by a gentle lady, he was left, not with a broken heart but with a chip on his shoulder.

It was Nancy, however, who re-opened their correspondence. She wrote to tell him, not without a certain pursing of the mouth one feels, that Jenny Clow had, in November, been delivered of a son and was threatening a writ. Burns wondered what else he could take on – 'God have mercy upon me! a poor, dammed, incautious, duped unfortunate fool...' He offered at once to take the boy, but Jenny refused to give him up. Burns wrote to Ainslie asking him to find Jenny for him and 'settle the matter with her' – just as he had done with May Cameron. Ainslie did so, and Burns turned to his business affairs in Edinburgh and Glasgow. He wrote to Lord Glencairn – 'I wish to get into the Excise; I am told that your Lordship's interest will easily procure me the grant from the Commissioners.' It did. But while pushing his own interests as hard as he could, he did not forget that he had a brother and sisters to fend for too. His letter to Glencairn continued –

My brother's lease [at Mossgiel] is a wretched one, though I think he will probably weather out the remaining seven years of it. After what I have given and will give him as a small farming capital to keep the family together... I will lodge my little stock, a sacred deposite, in a banking house –

But in order to carry out this sensible plan, he needed to get his money out of Creech. 'The miserable dunning and plaguing of Creech has busied me until I am good for nothing.' The delay was really getting him down for there was very little he could do about it – except persist in asking. 'Last week I wrote him a frosty, keen letter. He replied in terms of chastisement, and promised me upon his honor that I should have the account on Monday; but this is Tuesday, and yet I have not heard a word from him.' It was now the middle of February, and he had been waiting since the end of October. It was too much. John Grierson said that he knew a person who saw –

Burns coming up Leith Walk brandishing a sapling & with much violence in his face and manner. When asked what was the matter, Burns replied – 'I am going to smash that Shite Creech.

Fortunately, he was diverted or he might certainly have murdered the publisher. Creech could not publish enough of Burns, and would go on doing so, and yet he could not bring himself to finalise accounts. Burns mused: 'The question is not what door of fortune's palace shall we enter in: but what doors does she open to us?'

He went to Glasgow, to Paisley (A20), and then on to Tarbolton (A5) where he persuaded his good friends, the Muirs, to take in Jean, who was now in fear of her father's anger. In an unworthy letter to Nancy, Burns explained that despite this act, despite the fact that she was again carrying his child and was almost at her time –

> I am disgusted with her; I cannot endure her! I, while my heart smote me for the prophanity, tried to compare her with my Clarinda; 'twas setting the expiring glimmer of a farthing taper beside the cloudless glory of the meridian sun – here was tasteless insipidity, vulgarity of soul, and mercenary fawning; there polished good sense, heaven-born genius, and the most generous, the most delicate, the most tender Passion – I have done with her, and she with me.

One can only think that he was carried away with words. It was the poet speaking, not the man.

It was a very different letter he sent to Ainslie not long afterwards – this was not the man, but the braggart – carried away again:

> I found Jean banished like a martyr – forlorn, destitute and friendless. All for the good old cause. I have reconciled her to her fate, and I have reconciled her to her mother. I have taken a room for her. I have taken her to my arms. I have given her a mahogany bed. I have given her a guinea. And I have fucked her till she rejoiced with joy unspeakable and full of glory...Oh, what a peacemaker is a guid, weely-wally pintle! It is the mediator, the umpire, the bond of union, the solemn league and covenant, the plenipotentiary, the Aaron's rod, the Jacob's staff, the prophet Elisha's pot of oil, the Ahasueraus' Sceptre, the sword of mercy, the philosopher's stone, the Horn of Plenty, and Tree of Life between Man and Woman.

However much it may have titillated Ainslie, it shows Burns at his worst – but one can only think he was drunk at the time. On the other hand, he may have been trying to conceal the fact – for his Excise hopes – that Jean was pregnant. Whatever the reason, it was a painful episode for all concerned.

Jean was delivered of twins less than a week later – 9 March 1788 – and both died soon after. Burns had already left for Glasgow on that very day and was back in Edinburgh by 13th and was once again writing to Creech – '...such a letter, that the very goosefeather in my hand shrunk back from the line...' It was not until the 19th that Burns got his statement and his money. He also had in his pocket his Excise Commission after undergoing the necessary training and 'supping with the Principals', and finally, he had agreed a bargain with Patrick Miller about his farm at Ellisland. Everything at last was in order and he could leave Edinburgh and go home. He had achieved everything he had come for – except a wife. The only thing left now was to part from his pen-pal, Clarinda. His last letter to Nancy was written on 18 March, after they had dined at the White Hart Inn (B13) and he had walked her home. He wrote:

> The walk – delightful; the evening – rapture; do not be uneasy today, Clarinda; forgive me.

Uneasy about what? Whatever it was, Sylvander took his final bow with Clarinda and the curtain came down in Arcady.

When, in January 1792, she was leaving on the *Roselle* (the very ship in which Burns himself had booked passage in 1786), in order to join her husband in Jamaica, she received a song from Burns as a parting gift. This work, hurriedly scrawled on a card from Sanquhar Post Office (A27), was a poignant declaration of what Dr Maurice Lindsay called 'a resigned passion' and worth more than all the fifty-two letters he had written to her. This was Burns speaking and not Sylvander.

Ae fond kiss, and then we sever!
Ae fareweel, and then forever!
Deep in heart-wrung tears I'll pledge thee,
Warring sighs and groans I'll wage thee.
Who shall say that Fortune grieves him,
While the Star of Hope she leaves him?
Me, nae cheerfu' twinkle lights me,
Dark despair around benights me.
I'll ne'er blame my partial fancy;
Naething could resist my Nancy!
Just to see her was to love her,
Love but her and love forever.
Had we never lov'd sae kindly,
Had we never lov'd sae blindly,
Never met or never parted,
We had ne'er been broken hearted.

Fare-thee-weel, though first and fairest.
Fare-thee-weel, thou best and dearest;
Thine be ilka joy and treasure,
Peace, enjoyment, love and pleasure.
Ae fond kiss, and then we sever.
Ae fareweel, alas! Forever.

The whole, rather silly, brittle, self-conscious business, as Dr Lindsay implies, was worth it if only for this song. It is extraordinary that it was written on the back of a card and posted hurriedly from a country post office in Sanquhar, just as we today might write a card on holiday saying to a friend – a dear friend – 'Wish You Were Here'. Genius is by its very nature unusual, but it is a singular thing that Burns so often seems to catch an emotion in a flash, as if he were taking a photograph of the feeling, and there it is, caught for ever. No doubt Nancy would read it again and again. In her journal for 6 December 1831, she noted –

This day parted from my Sylvander, never to meet again on this earth.
O, that we might meet in Heaven.

In a white-gabled house in the Low Calton (B15), that part of Edinburgh lying under the Calton Hill,' comforted by her surviving son, Andrew, an old lady lived out her long, remaining years. She kept the famous letters in a small, oblong box covered in cheap wallpaper, and would often take them out to look them over.

The years saw all passion die away
And fade into the light of common day.

When she herself died in 1841, on the orders of her grandson the box of letters was put up for auction at the offices of C.B.Tait and Company of Hanover Street, and was sold for only a few shillings – 'being the value of the box'.

CHAPTER 7

Ellisland

To make a happy, fireside clime to weans and wife
That is the true pathos, and sublime, of human life.

GIVEN AT MAUCHLINE, in early April 1788:

BE IT KNOWN that Jean Armour is installed into all the
rights and privileges, immunities, franchises and parapher-
nalia that at present do, or at any time may, belong to the
name, title and designation – WIFE of Robert Burns, Poet.

The marriage of Robert Burns and Jean Armour in Gavin
Hamilton's office in Mauchline may have been irregular but it was
legal, having been declared before John Farquhar-Gray of
Gilmanscroft, a recognised magistrate. It was a step the patient Jean
deserved, as she had regarded herself as wife to Burns from the
beginning of their relationship, but Burns was, as ever, keen to take
the credit. As he wrote to Peggy Chalmers a few days later – 'I have
lately made some sacrifices for which, were I *viva voce* with you to
paint the situation and recount the circumstances, you would
applaud me...' The fact was that he and Jean had long ago made their
bed and now they had to lie on it. Jean had got the husband she
wanted and he had got a better wife than he knew. He gave her a
printed shawl and 'entitlement to the best blood in my body – so
farewell Rakery!' Or, as the old Scots saying has it –

Bode a robe and wear it;
Bode a pock, and bear it.

The Mauchline Kirk Session eventually gave its approval to
the match and it also recorded that 'Mr Burns gave a guinea-note
for the behoof of the poor'.

In addition to this confirmed matrimonial status, he now had
a triple part to play in the outside world – as part-time farmer,

part-time exciseman and part-time poet. It was a situation which meant in reality that he could not give proper time to any of these demands. Yet the *Edinburgh Advertiser* of 28 November 1788, could print:

Burns, the Ayrshire Bard, is now enjoying the fruits of his retirement at his farm in Dumfries. Burns, in thus retiring, has acted wisely. Stephen Duck, the poetical thresher, by his ill-advised patrons, was made a parson. The poor man, hurried out of his proper element, found himself quite unhappy, became insane, and with his own hands ended his life. Burns, with propriety, has resumed the flail – but, we hope, has not thrown away the quill.

The sheer impertinence of comparing the aptly-named Duck with such as Burns merits scant comment except to underline how little Edinburgh society appreciated the power of the literary comet that had so recently blazed over Auld Reekie. As far as they were concerned, he had reverted to his proper status. It would have been nice, and no less deserved, if *his* patrons had been able to find him the equivalent of thresher Duck's parsonage, where he could have happily written his remaining years away. There was talk of a sinecure at the Salt Office in Leith, but nothing came of it.

This ought to have been the time when someone made a move to regularize his editorship of the musical volumes, but nothing was done there either, so he was forced back on his own measures and that meant having his nose rubbed in the dirt of farming yet again, with the hope of some extras to be picked up through the Excise. Whichever way he turned, he had a hard furrow to hoe, but then, when was it ever easy for him? He had had his excursions and his fame, his hour in the sun. It was time to get back to cold, stern, Scottish reality. His tours now would extend to that area of Nithsdale that was in his Excise Division, and his halts would be at inns and farms instead of mansions and castles. Meantime, he had a farmhouse of his own to build.

I have taken a farm on the banks of the Nith and in imitation of the old Patriarchs, I shall have men servants and maid servants, flocks and herds and beget sons and daughters.

The farm was on the west bank of the river in the parish of Dunscore and just over five miles from Dumfries. It comprised 170 acres but had no suitable house. The farm may have had poetic views but it was badly run down. Burns would have his work cut out to make it a going concern, and he knew it. It had potential, but the first signs were not promising. Old Glenconner, his father's friend from Alloway days, had advised him to take it, on condition that he was willing to work it. If he did, he might turn it round, but Burns, with everything else he heaped on his plate, never gave more than a divided mind to it, and the results were inevitable. Despite his premonitions, he had committed himself to 'sober science' and, at the time, was convinced that he could do it, God willing. God, however, was perhaps more willing than Burns was, even though he had signed a lease for the next 76 years. Jean, meantime, went to live at Mossgiel to be with her son and learn a farmwife's duties from Mrs Burnes and the sisters, while her new husband went on alone to make the farmhouse habitable. Till then he would commute between Ayrshire and Dumfries. He had little time for thoughts of songs or verses now.

I am so harassed by Care and Anxiety about this farming project of mine, that my Muse has degenerated into the veriest prose-wench that ever picked cinders, or followed a Tinker.

Just in case, he began a further course of instruction in the Excise at Tarbolton (A5) in April. In May, he received the final instalment of a hundred guineas on his copyright. This was just as well, as he was to need every shilling of it. He completed his instruction and at Whitsunday 1788 took over officially as farmer at Ellisland. But it was to be Martinmas (11 November) of the following year before Burns could move 'bag and baggage' on to the farm. Until then, the year ahead was to be one long slog to enable him to bring Jean and Robert to Dumfries, not to mention 'men servants, maid servants, flocks and herds'. The 'sons and daughters' would come in their own time. He was enjoying a blissful honeymoon period with Jean in the times he did see her. Whenever he was due at Mossgiel, she would walk to the road end to meet him, and they would walk back to the house together. He only wrote four letters to Jean in his life, but they were a far cry from the posturings of 1787. For instance, on 12 September –

I received your kind letter with a pleasure no letter but one from you could have given me – I dreamed of you the whole night last; but alas! I fear it will be three weeks yet, ere I can hope for the happiness of seeing you. My harvest is going on. I have some to cut down still, but I put in two stacks today, so I am as tired as a dog...

This was the new husbandman, Burns, in every sense of the word. He couldn't wait for their own house to be finished, so he arranged for the use of Mr Newall's empty house nearby – a very happy arrangement for all concerned during that first, long, hard winter. He also got himself a new horse, Pegasus, and was almost ready for the new phase. Jean had arrived with a companion-cum-help from Mauchline (A7), Elizabeth Smith, and it was she who left us a picture of the move to the new farmhouse when it was finally ready by the end of April 1789. Burns told her to carry the Bible and a bowl of salt – 'and placing one upon the other, carry them to the new house, and walk into it before anyone else'. Burns followed arm in arm with Jean. This ceremony of the book and the salt was the ancient *freit* where the Word of God and the Staff of Life were supposed to bring luck to the new house and its first tenant. Luck was something Burns had never known on any of the three farms he had worked in his life, but he was full of a whole new resolve, determined to turn over a new leaf as much as any new soil. He genuinely felt he was starting again, and at 30 years of age considered he still had plenty of time.

I have dallied long enough with life. And a wife and children soon show that a bachelor's most anxious moments are spent on trifles.

Yet he was never too far from trifling opportunities. What engaged him next was not a farm scheme but an unexpected poetic one, which would not only confirm his genius but justify the whole move to Ellisland. His only travelling, apart from his rounds, and visits to Dumfries (A23) or Sanquhar (A27) for his letters, was a flight of the imagination which would provide him with his masterpiece.

In that summer of 1789 he had made friends with Captain Robert Riddell and his family, who were his next-door neighbours on their Friars' Carse estate. Through them he met with a certain Captain Francis Grose, who was, in a sense, responsible for Burns's greatest work. Grose, described by Burns as 'a cheerful-looking grig of an old fat fellow...wheeling about in his own carriage with a pencil and paper in his hand', was touring the country looking for interesting sites to include in his proposed *Antiquities of Scotland*, having already published a volume on the *Antiquities of England and Wales*. Burns suggested he look at Alloway Kirk (A1), and Grose said he would include it if Burns would supply a story to go with it. Burns eventually gave him three tales about the old Kirk, all of which had something of the genesis of the subsequent *Tam o' Shanter* story. These were tales that Burns had imbibed almost subconsciously from the Ayrshire folk he had known from boyhood and he took this opportunity to write them out, probably for the first time, for the benefit of his new friend.

> Among the many witch-stories I have heard relating to Alloway Kirk, I distinctly remember only two or three. The first concerned a farmer, or farmer's servant, who was plodding and plashing homeward with his plough-irons on his shoulder, having been getting repairs of them at a neighbouring smithy' when he was struck aghast by discovering through the horrors of [a] storm, a light, which...plainly shewed itself to proceed from the haunted edifice. Whether fortified by prayer or drink, or impelled by mere curiosity, he ventured nearer. He saw a kind of kettle or cauldron, depending from the roof over a fire, simmering some heads of unchristened children, limbs of executed malefactors, etc...Without ceremony, the honest ploughman, unhooked the cauldron from the fire, and pouring out the damnable ingredients, inverted on his head, and carried it fairly home, where it remained long in his family, a living evidence of the truth of the story.

The second story dealt with a Carrick farmer who came back from Ayr market by way of Alloway Kirk at what Burns called the 'wizard hour between night and morning'.

> He was surprised and entertained to see a dance of witches merrily foot-

ing it round their old sooty blackguard master, who was keeping them all alive by the sound of his bagpipe. The farmer, stopping his horse to observe them closer could plainly descry the faces of many old women of his acquaintance...all in their smocks: and one of them happening unluckily to have a smock which was considerably too short to answer the purpose of that dress...Our farmer was so tickled by this sight that he involuntarily burst out 'Weel luppen, Maggie, wi' the short sark!' Then, recollecting himself he instantly spurred his horse to the top of his speed. Luckily the bridge of the River Doon was near, and it is universally known that no diabolical power can pursue you beyond the middle of a running stream...When he reached the arch of the bridge, one of the vengeful hags actually sprang to seize him - but it was too late; nothing was on her side of the stream but the horse's tail, which immediately gave way at her infernal grip, as if blasted by a stroke of lightning; the farmer was beyond her reach...but the tail-less condition of that vigorous steed remained to the last hour of his life an awful warning to Carrick farmers not to stay too late in Ayr markets.

Burns insisted that the final tale was 'equally true' and he had it from the 'best authorities in Ayrshire'. This was the story of a shepherd boy –

who fell in with a crew of men and women busily pulling stems of rag-wort...and when they got astride of [them,] they called out 'Up horsie!' and flew up like Pegasus through the air. The foolish boy cried 'Up horsie!' with the rest, and, strange to tell, away he flew with the company. The cavalcade stopt at Bordeaux, where...they quaffed away at the merchant's best cellar until the morning. The poor shepherd boy, being equally a stranger to the scene and to liquor, got himself hopelessly drunk; and when the rest took to horse, he fell asleep and was found next day by the merchant, and by somebody who understood Scotch. By some means or other he got home and lived long enough to tell the world this wondrous tale.

These then were the disparate strands which Burns took to weave his own particular narrative. He also added the real-life figure of Robert Graham, a tenant of the farm of Shanter on Carrick shore, who owned a boat called the *Tam o'Shanter* (which Burns might have known at Kirkoswald (A3) and had a wife Kate who was famous for her temper. Tradition has it that Graham's horse, a long-tailed grey mare, had waited longer than usual for her master at the tavern door, and 'certain humourists plucked her tail to such an extent so as to leave it little better than a stump'.

It is not known what turned Burns from prose to poetry with these tales, but the gregarious Grose had first met Burns at dinner and no doubt he wanted the same sparkle and wit that marked the Scot's convivial conversation, and he might well have suggested that he work the material 'to his own voice'. Or it may have been just another Burns whim to work in rhyme. After all, that's what he knew best. Whatever the motive, he took his time getting down to it. He had started on the project during 1789, but it was not till a year later that he finished it. The final poetic mix of 229 octosyllabic lines was given the motto from the medieval poet, Gavin Douglas – '*Of brownies and bogillis full is this book*' – then Tam was ready to ride his faithful Maggie into legend. Burns sent it to Grose on 1 December 1790, saying:

Should you think it worthy a place in your Scots Antiquities, it will lengthen not a little, the altitude of my Muse's pride.

Grose acknowledged his debt to Burns when his book was published in April 1791:

To my ingenious friend, Robert Burns, I have been seriously obligated; he was not only at the pains of making out what was worthy of most notice in Ayrshire, the county honoured by his birth, but he also wrote, expressly for this work, the pretty tale annexed to Alloway Church.

Lockhart, on Cromek's authority, accepts Jean Armour's recollection that the poem was the work of a single day ('from breakfast till dinner-time') but one must bear in mind that Burns himself said, 'All my poetry has the effect of easy composition, but is the result of laborious correction'. There speaks the professional. Jean cannot be blamed for believing that it had been written from start to finish in that November day at Ellisland. She remembered that Burns had been seen by William Clark, their labourer, 'stridin' up an' doon the broo o' the Scaur, recitin' tae himsel' like ane dementit'. He ran to tell Mrs Burns, but she told him to leave Mr Burns alone: 'He's best on his lane when the mood is on him.'

When later it began to rain heavily, it was she who had to go out to him. She found him sheltering under a tree, where he was sitting with a paper in his hand and laughing his head off. When she persuaded him to come in, he was declaiming loudly –

Now Tam! O, Tam! had thae been queans,
A' plump and strapping in their teens!
Their sarks, instead of creeshie flannen,
Been snaw-white, seventeen-hunner linen! -
Thir breeks o' mine, my only pair,
That ance were plush, o' gude, blue hair,
I wad hae gi'en them aff my hurdies
For ae blink o' the bonie burdies!

He recited it first to his family and the servants before his own fireside, and it is said that he so frightened the children that they hid under the table. His own verdict on the work was given to Mrs Dunlop in April 1791 when in a letter to her he said that 'it showed a finishing polish...which I despair of ever excelling'. And again – 'I look on *Tam o' Shanter* to be my standard performance in the poetical line.'

If Burns had written nothing else, *Tam o' Shanter* would have assured his immortality. It places him unreservedly in the first rank of poetical writers. Not since *The Jolly Beggars*, five years earlier, and, to a lesser extent, *Holy Willie's Prayer*, had the lines leapt from the page, so alive and exultant. Nor had his dramatic instinct emerged as clearly as it does in this tale of one man's drunken adventure. The piece surges with linguistic certainty, both in Scots and English, and the unerring rhythmic detail conjures up for the reader those vivid pictures in the mind that are the mark of complete narrative artistry. The work flows on with a seeming ease that only underlines the workmanship that such spontaneity conceals. It is a seamless garment of words that cloaks a series of events, both comic and horrifying. It is a work that has all the best of Burns in it – his wit and wisdom, comic invention, humour and humanity, warmth of character, and, above all, a searing observation that makes everything and everyone believable, even Satan himself. The whole thing goes at a gallop, literally, and the pace is developed to a thrilling conclusion. We are carried along with Tam the whole way, and when he leaps the Brig o' Doon, we leap with him in an imaginative jump that lifts us into high art. It is a work that emerges from the crucible of the poet's mind, white-hot and brimming with energy. It needed little hammering or tempering to make it ring true. There is no evidence of 'laborious correction', it comes from the furnace ready-made and right. One can well believe the impact it made on that little family group that night. It has hung like a star over Ellisland ever since. He was never to write anything as considerable again.

Ellisland was already proving 'a ruinous bargain'. 'Let it go to Hell!' he said. 'I'll fight it off and be done with it.' To offset the dreary drudge that farming had become for him, he began to have 'some thoughts on the drama'. Just as he had taken to the Bible when laid up with his injured knee at St James Square (B10) in Edinburgh, so now he took to Shakespeare and pondered on theatre. Professional companies came to Dumfries (A23) and, in the absence of a proper theatre, played at the Assembly Rooms in George Street. Proposals were put forward to build a replica of the Theatre Royal, Bristol, in Dumfries, by subscription. Burns did not subscribe, but on Hogmanay 1789 he had written to George Sutherland, the manager of the theatre company:

> Jogging home yesternight, it occurred to me that as your next night is the first night of the New Year, a few lines allusive to the Season by way of Prologue, Interlude or what you please, might take very well... I shall not be in the least mortified though if they are never heard of no more, but if they can be of any service...

Prologue to be spoken New Year's Day Evening at the Theatre of Dumfries:

No song nor dance, I bring from yon great city
That queens it o'er our taste, the more's the pity!
Tho, by the by, abroad why will you roam?
Good sense and taste are natives here at home.
But not for panegyric I appear,
I come to wish you all a good New Year!
Old Father Time deputes me here before ye

Not for to preach, but tell his simple story.
The sage, grave, Ancient cough'd, and bade me say:
'You're one day older this important day'.
If wiser too, he hinted some suggestion,
But 'twould be rude, you know, to ask the question;
And with a would-be-roguish leer and wink
He bade me press this one word – think!
Ye sprightly youths, quite flush with hope and spirit,
Who think to storm the world by dint of merit,
To you, the dotard has a deal to say,
In his sly, dry, sententious proverb way!
He bids you mind, among your thoughtless rattle,
That the first blow is ever half the battle;
Yet by the forelock is the hold to catch him;
That, whether doing, suffering or forbearing,
We may do miracles by persevering.
Last, tho' not in least in love, ye youthfu' fair,
Angelic forms, high Heaven's peculiar care!
To you, Bald-pate smoothes his wrinkled brow,
And humbly begs you'll mind the important – now!
To crown your happiness, he asks your leave,
And offers bliss, to give and to receive.
For our sincere, tho' haply, weak endeavours,
With grateful pride, we own your many favours;
And, howsoe'er our tongues may ill-reveal it,
Believe our glowing bosoms truly feel it.'

No matter the conventional artificiality of the style, there is a Burnsian grit in it and you can be sure that there is more genuine philosophical worth displayed here than in many of the plays of the time then presented by Mr Sutherland's theatre company. The Prologue was published in several newspapers soon afterwards.

Burns continued to take a keen interest in the players. This can be seen in his letter to Wille Nicol, dated 2 February 1790:

Our theatrical company, of which you must have heard, leave us in a week. Their merit and character are indeed very great, both on stage and in private life; not a worthless creature among them; and their encouragement has been accordingly. Their usual run is from eighteen to twenty five pounds a night, seldom less than one and the house will not take more than the other. There have been repeated instances of sending away, six, and eight, and ten pounds in a night for want of room. A new theatre is to be built by subscription; the first stone to be laid on Friday first to come. Three hundred guineas have been raised by thirty subscribers and thirty more might have been got if wanted. The manager was introduced to me by a friend from Ayr; and a worthier or cleverer fellow I never met with. Some of our clergy have slipped in by stealth now and then.

Burns had been put on the free list by Sutherland, and, as far as his farming and Excise duties allowed, he was a regular at all first nights. He repaid the manager's generosity with further Addresses and Prologues, and when Mrs Sutherland was due her benefit night, Burns obliged as usual. However, given the times, and as he felt there was a *dark stroke of Politics in the belly of the Piece*', he felt it necessary to first run it past a local magistrate, Provost Staig, and then likewise, his social mentor, Mrs Dunlop – just in case. Neither objected, so Mrs Sutherland said her piece:

A Scots Prologue For Mrs Sutherland On Her Benefit Night At The Theatre:

What needs this din about the town o' Lon'on,
How this new play and that new sang is comin'?
Why is outlandish stuff sae meikle courted?
Does nonsense mend, like brandy, when imported?
Is there nae poet, burning keen for fame,
Will bauldly try to gie us plays at hame?
For Comedy abroad he needna toil;
A knave and fool are plants of every soil.
Nor need he hunt as far as Rome or Greece
To gather matter for a serious piece;
There's themes enow in Caledonia's story
Wad show the Tragic Muse in a' her glory.
Is there no daring bard will rise and tell
How glorious Wallace stood, how hapless fell?
Where are the Muses fled that could produce

A Drama worthy o' the name o' Bruce?
How here, even here, he first unsheath'd the sword
Gainst mighty England and her mighty lord,
And after many a deathless doing
Wrench'd his dear country from the jaws of Ruin!
O, for a Shakespeare or an Otway scene
To paint, the lovely, hapless, Scottish Queen!
Vain all th'omnipotence of female charms
'Gainst headlong, ruthless, mad Rebellion's arms!
She fell, but fell with spirit truly Roman,
To glut the vengeance of a rival woman:
A woman, tho' the phrase may seem uncivil,
As able – and as cruel – as the Devil!
One Douglas lives in Home's immortal page,
But Douglases were heroes every age;
And, though your fathers, prodigal of life,
A Douglas followed to the martial strife,
Perhaps, if bowls row right, the Right succeeds,
Ye yet may follow where a Douglas leads!
As ye hae generations done, if a' the land
Wad take the Muse's servants by the hand;
Not only hear, but patronise, befriend them,
And where ye justly can commend, commend them,
And aiblins, when they winna stand the test,
Wink hard, and say, 'The folks hae done their best!'
Would a' the lands do this, then I'll be caition,
Ye'll soon hae poets o' the Scottish nation
Will gar Fame blaw until her trumpet crack,
And warsle Time an' lay him on his back!
For us, and for our stage, should onie spier –
'Whase aught thae chiels maks a' this bustle here?'
My best leg foremost, I'll set up my broo –
'We have the honour to belong to you!'
We're your ain bairns, e'en guide us as ye like,
But, like good mothers, shore before ye strike;
And gratefu' still, I trust you' ever find us,
For gen'rous patronage, and meikle kindness

We've got frae a' professions, setts, an' ranks;
God help us! We're but poor – ye'se get but thanks!

This is more than a *cri de coeur* for patronage from the actors
to the audience, it is the first call on record for the establishment
of a National Drama in Scotland. Burns has not been given the
credit for this. Given these various Prologues, it is a wonder that
neither Woods in Edinburgh, nor Sutherland here, ever suggested
to Burns that he might write a play for them.

Of course it may be that it just never occurred to them. Burns
was so evident a poet that the writing of prologues and addresses
would be, to them, the full extent of his dramatic range. It must
be admitted too, that his theatrical knowledge, up until his
Edinburgh and Dumfries times, was limited to a reading of plays,
play-scenes and speeches from plays – and a positive devouring of
Shakespeare. DeLancey Ferguson points out that in the Burns
Letters there are 26 quotations from 9 of the plays, and even more
in the poems. In the same article, *Burns and the Drama*, he adds
the comment that some of the unidentified quotes were obviously
of dramatic origin.

Burns came to his first plays through the English editor, Arthur
Masson's *Collection of Prose and Verse from the Best English
Authors*. This was a rich feeding ground for a book-minded boy
with ambitions to work with words. Given this kind of introduction to drama, how else could he think of a play but as a vehicle
for ringing speeches and telling phrases. If he was influenced by
Scottish contemporary theatre at all, it was by a kind of drama
like Allan Ramsay's *Gentle Shepherd* of 1725 and John Home's
Douglas of 1756 which was still fashionable from generations
before.

Burns was never given a sense of the *machinery* of playmak-
ing, or the sheer practise of theatre. As every playwright since
Shakespeare has found, this can only be learned by doing it, and
he was given no opportunity for doing so. Yet thoughts of the
stage kept niggling him at Ellisland. Even with all his other preoccupations, he actually voiced his dramatic ideas in a letter to
Graham of Fintry:

> I am thinking of something in the rural way of the Drama-kind. Originality of character is, I think, the most striking beauty in that species of composition, and my wanderings in the way of business would be vastly favourable to my picking up original traits of Human Nature...

There could be nothing plainer than this. He was telling the world that he wanted to write a play, and like the shrewd craftsman he was, he knew he had all the material he wanted right to hand. He would write about what he knew best, the life and times of the characters he met in the course of every working day. There were no gods here, or classical beings, or supernatural images, just the matter and manner of the everyday which, as a poet, he knew to be unique in each living person involved. Somehow one feels, contrary to DeLancey Ferguson and others, that Burns would have scorned ancient deeds fleshed out with fustian speeches. He always kept his ears and eyes open. That is what gave him his poetic reservoir. There is no reason why it could not have given him the dramatic equivalent. He told us in his first Commonplace Book that he was going to write poems and songs. Now he is saying he is going to write a play. Unfortunately, despite his success with the dramatic monologue (*Holy Willie's Prayer*) and the dramatic duologue (*The Twa Dugs*), he never did venture on his proposed play. Even Walter Scott had his pretentious *The Doom of Devergoil*, and Wordsworth his dull *The Borderers*, but the mercurial Burns gave us nothing approaching a play except *The Jolly Beggars* and *Tam o' Shanter*. We should be grateful for such large mercies.

Bob Ainslie visited in October 1790 and duly reported to Nancy McLehose:

> Our friend is as ingenious as ever...His mind, however, seems to be a great mixture of the poet and the excise-man. One day he sits down to write a beautiful poem – and the next seize a cargo of tobacco from an unfortunate smuggler...From his conversation he seems to be frequently among the Great...Having found his farm is not to answer, he is about to give it up and depend wholly on the Excise...

Burns had recently been listed for promotion to Supervisor so

Entrance to the Globe Inn

it seemed a sensible move to give up the farm, if only to cut down on the amount of riding he had to do in a week in all weathers, not to mention his nights away from home. With his increasing Excise responsibilities (he had lately been appointed Examiner, the step before Supervisor) and with the need to spend more time in Dumfries, he became a regular at the Globe Inn there – and at the Globe Inn was Anna Park.

Helen Anne Park was a relative of the proprietors of the Globe, Mr and Mrs William Hyslop, and she had come from Edinburgh to work as a barmaid at the Inn just when Burns first frequented the place. She was nineteen, blonde and susceptible, so the inevitable happened as soon as she met Burns. He made a song about her. *Yestreen I had a pint o' wine* is one of his best love songs, even if its direct earthiness offended its first publisher, George Thomson, who well knew its provenance. Burns had to write an expurgated version for publication. This affair with 'Anna of the Gowden Locks' was Burns's only infidelity with Jean after their marriage. Agnes Burns, his spinster sister, who was at Ellisland at the time, remembers that Jean was at Mauchline (A7) visiting her people when Burns became involved with the blonde barmaid.

The summer affair ran its natural course but not before Anna was pregnant. Once again, Burns's twin curse had been proved - barren soil and fertile women. As he could never succeed with a farm it would appear he could never fail with a woman. By the time Jean returned to Ellisland, Burns was staying at home nursing a broken arm as a result of a fall from his horse. Early in 1791, Anna left for Edinburgh where she would have a daughter on 31 March. Jean would have her third son, William Nicol Burns, almost exactly a month later. No one is certain what happened to Anna herself after the delivery, but her child came to Mossgiel and from there to Ellisland – to be cared for by Jean. It was at this time she made her famous remark – 'Oor Robin should hae had twa wives'.

His virility may never have been in question, but his health generally was worrying Burns. He wrote to Gilbert: 'My nerves are in a damnable state – I feel that horrid hypochondria pervading every atom of both body and soul...' It was clear that he could not go on like this and something had to go. He decided it had to be Ellisland with its 'riddlings of creation' – his first suspicions had been proved right. He made plans to move his whole family into Dumfries. Catherine Carswell, in her 1930 account of Burns's life, has the telling aphorism – 'A man's failure is doubled when he fails under the eyes of his wife'. One must wonder what exactly Jean did say to her husband after the failure of Ellisland. She knew his other preoccupations better than any. This private, domestic Burns is underplayed too often, but one can be sure that it was a very different Burns to the public figure. Notwithstanding, the decision to leave was made, and on 25 August 1791 the last crops and farming effects were auctioned off and some thirty persons turned up to see if they could get a bit of Poet Burns. Burns himself described the action:

Such a scene of drunkenness was hardly ever seen in this country. Nor was the scene much better in the house. No fighting indeed, but folk lying drunk on the floor & decanting, until both dogs got so drunk by attending them, that they could not stand...

Burns turned his back on it all, on the land, and on his previous thirty-one years. It was time to turn over yet another leaf. And so, on 11 November 1791, he led his family to begin a new life in the town. The family now consisted of Robert and Jean, and sons Robert (4), Francis (2) and William (8 months), as well as Elizabeth Park, Anna Park's daughter by Burns. She had been given her place in the cart as it took all of them and their possessions the five-and-three-quarter miles into Dumfries. The only reminder of their country life was Jean's milk cow, which trailed on a rope behind them...

CHAPTER 8

Dumfries (1791 - 1794)

Envy, if thy jaundiced eye
Through this window chance to spy,
To thy sorrow thou shalt find
All that's generous, all that's kind –
Friendship, virtue, every grace
Dwelling in this happy place.

HAPPINESS WAS OFTEN SHY of Robert Burns. Perhaps in the early Lochlie years, and in the miraculous Mossgiel surge of 1785/86, in occasional love exchanges, in Masonic hours and in moments during his high celebrity, he was to know a sense of elation and fulfilment, but otherwise Robert Burns never had it easy. He may be said to have matured, artistically at least, during his Ellisland tenure. It was his second great creative period, begun by the eruption of the volcanic *Tam o' Shanter* and culminating in a wave of great songs. He had also become something of a tourist attraction on his farm. Visitors from every part found a way to his door, so a retreat from such a conspicuous profile was also something to be gained from lying low as Citizen Burns in Dumfries (A23). After all, he was a Burgher of the town and the publicly proclaimed Bard of All Scotland. He had something to bring with him other than a cartload of chattels and children.

Burns House Museum, Dumfries

His impact on Dumfries over the next five years is shown today in the number of Burns places associated with the poet. There are probably more sites, stones, relics, statues, busts, etc, relating to Burn here than anywhere else in the world - certainly more than Ayr (A2) or Kilmarnock (A8) or any of the other recognised

Burns shrines. One has merely to walk through Dumfries and Burns is pressing in on one from every side. This is as it should be in a place so heavily associated with him, yet the irony is (and how much in his life is ironical) that it was in Dumfries he reputedly touched his lowest ebb. How true this is we shall see, but it is certainly a fact that when he was at the very height of his creative powers he was at the near-nadir of his personal life.

When he had installed Jean and the four children in the three rooms above John Syme's law office in the Wee Vennel and paid his first rent to his landlord, Captain Hamilton, almost the first letter he received was from Mrs McLehose. She was now back in Edinburgh, having crossed the Atlantic to Jamaica, only to find James McLehose ensconced with his 'dark lady'. Nancy immediately turned on her heel and went back to the ship to wait until it sailed back to Scotland. Now she was writing to Burns to tell him that Jenny Clow was destitute and dying – 'I need add nothing further to act as every consideration of humanity, as well as gratitude must dictate...' Burns replied at once – 'It is extremely difficult, my dear Madam, for me to deny a lady anything...' He asked her to send five shillings in his name.

Burns made no mention this time of Jenny's son, now aged three. Perhaps he thought Jean might have had her hands full as it was. Jenny's Robert Burns the Second did well, no matter, and prospered as a merchant in London. His son, also called Robert, went to the East Indies and became a highly successful trader. Unfortunately, in 1851, his schooner, the *Dolphin*, was captured by pirates off the coast of Borneo and he was murdered with all of his crew. His descendants are to be found in the Far East to this day – a long way from that attic room in chilly Edinburgh's St James's Square (B10).

It is a curious fact that, when Burns first arrived in Dumfries three years before from the Border tour, he had found a letter on the same kind of business awaiting him from May Cameron. May thereafter disappeared, and now Jenny was dead. He had also taken his formal farewell of Nancy, but in 1791, having finished with one young lady of beauty, education and refinement, he immediately took up with another.

Maria Riddell was eighteen years old when Burns met her first at Friars' Carse. She was the extremely beautiful wife of the rich but dull Walter Riddell, brother to Robert Riddell, Burns's good friend and Ellisland neighbour. Burns was immediately drawn to her. She was just the type of the society women he admired – like Peggy Chalmers – witty, lively and well-read, and like Nancy Mclehose, Maria was also a writer. She was not a poet, but a writer of respectable prose. In all, a formidable young woman. Her account of her stay in the West Indies, *Voyages to the Madeira and Leeward Caribee Islands,* was admired by no less than William Smellie, to whom Burns gave her an introduction when she visited her husband's relatives in Edinburgh.

> Mrs Riddell, who takes this letter to town with her is a Character that, even in your own way as a Naturalist and Philosopher, would be an acquisition to your acquaintance...lest you should think of a lively West-Indian girl of eighteen, as girls of eighteen too often deserve to be thought of, I should take care to remove that prejudice...She has one failing – where she dislikes or despises, she is apt to make no more a secret of it – than where she esteems...

Burns was to find out how true this was. Smellie, however, was so impressed by the author as well as the work that he printed the volume and the two became real friends thereafter. This then was the new woman in Burns's life, not to depose Jean – no one would do that now – but to co-exist with her. A tuppence-coloured dream to her practical, penny-plain reality. Jean was right after all, Burns really needed two wives – one as a Muse and the other as the keeper of his body. If Maria was to be his focus for polite society in the Dumfries area, Jean was the one he always went home to.

And to this new home in the Wee Vennell he now returned to take up his duties in the Port Division. He made a colourful, if apocryphal, beginning in his new job if the *Edinburgh Courant* of 8 March 1792 is to be believed. It carried the story of how Burns, with the help of a company of Dragoons, captured the French schooner, *Rosamonde*, as it lay off the Solway coast. By assuming command of a raiding party, and by dint of some schoolroom French, he brought the ship and its crew into Dumfries harbour and was hailed as a hero. However, at the public auction of the ship's effects next day, he bought her four guns and returned them to the rebels of the French Convention with his poet's compliments. It was hardly the action of a Crown servant but it was just right for Burns.

Burns scholars have quarrelled for years about this anecdote. Lockhart says it's true, Snyder calls it 'pure Gilbert and Sullivan' and Dr James Mackay considers it 'not proven'. So we might leave it at that. It's still a good story. Stories grew up around Burns in his lifetime because he was that kind of man – colourful, charismatic, vulnerable and unthinking. This was sadly evident when he died. He may have been all things to all men but he got a bad press when he died, mainly because he was the victim of gossip and hearsay, arising from the fear and jealousy of timid men who never knew him but heard from a man who knew a man who once saw Burns in the street – at the dockside – in the Globe Inn – or at the Theatre Royal.

The new Theatre Royal, (now the oldest theatre in Scotland, and featuring his bust on the interior wall), opened with much fanfare on 29 September 1792. The *Dumfries Weekly* reported that – 'It is allowed by persons of first taste and opportunities that this is the handsomest theatre in Scotland'. The architect is given as Thomas Boyd but a sketch of the backdrop which can be seen at the National Gallery of Scotland bears the legend – *'Design for the Dumfries Theatre, done at the request of Robert Burns, by Alexander Nasmyth'* – the very man who painted the portrait of Robert Burns seen on every biscuit tin and paper napkin to this day. Nasmyth held the same egalitarian views as Burns and had fallen on hard times as a result, and was glad of the commission. Burns should have taken warning from his friend's decline, but he was more concerned that Nasmyth received his hundred guineas fee. Burns showed the same concern for an actor in the company when he too needed help. He wrote to Provost Staig:

Among the company of players here there is one to whose merits as an actor you are no stranger; his name is Guion. Strolling Comedians are a class of folk with whom, you will readily believe, I wish to have very little communication. When Mr Guion came here, he was introduced to my acquaintance by a friend of mine in Edinburgh, a gentleman of distinguished character there who begged me to serve Guion in anything I could with propriety do. I have found Mr Guion to be truly what my friend represented him, a man of more than common information & worth. His benefit comes on tomorrow night – Now Sir – is there any periphrase of language, any circumlocution of phrase, in which I could convey a request, without, at the same time seeming to convey it, that your amiable Lady and lovely daughters would grace my friend, Mr Guion's Boxes? Such a petition I have no right to make – Nay, it is downright impertinence in me to make it.

But make it he did, and good for him for doing so. A more congenial task was to compose not only a Benefit-night Prologue, but an Address and Epigram for the new leading lady in the company, Louisa Fontanelle. London-born, she had played at Covent Garden and also in Edinburgh and Glasgow, where she joined Sutherland. She later married the manager of the new Theatre Royal, J.B.Williamson, and emigrated to America with him in the year Burns died. She herself died soon after in Charleston, South Carolina, but in 1792, she was the toast of provincial Dumfries.

There was no doubt that Burns was drawn to her. Most men were. On 22 November he sent her what amounted to a fan letter:

In such a bad world as ours, those who add to the scanty sum of our pleasures, are positively our Benefactors. To you, Madam, on our humble Dumfries boards, I have been more indebted for entertainment than ever I was in prouder theatres. Your charms as a woman would secure applause to the most indifferent actress, and your theatrical talents would secure admiration to the plainest figure. This, Madam, is not the unmeaning, or insidious compliment of the Frivolous or Interested. I pay it from the same honest impulse that the Sublime of Nature excites my admiration, or her beauties give me delight – will the foregoing lines be of any service to you on your approaching benefit-night...?

A few days later, he wrote again – a typically impulsive, spontaneous, unthinking Burnsian action which was to have unexpected and serious repercussions. Yet, at the time, he had no more than the theatrical in mind and the desire to please an artist he had admired from the stalls. He wrote:

I am thinking of sending my Address to some periodical publication, but it has not got your sanction, so pray look over it. As to Tuesday's play, let me beg of you, Madam, to give us The Wonder, to which please add The Spoilt Child. You will greatly oblige me by so doing...

Burns got his printing, and a whole heap of trouble. His desire to impress the actress had the very opposite effect on his superiors and the good citizens of Dumfries. The controversial lines duly appeared in the *Edinburgh Gazetteer* as follows:

The Rights of Women – An Occasional Address spoken on her Benefit-night, November 26th, at Dumfries by Miss Fontanelle. Written by Mr Burns.

While Europe's eyes are fix'd on mighty things,
The fate of empires and the fall of kings;
While quacks of State must each produce his plan
And even children lisp The Rights of Man;
Amid this mighty fuss, just let me mention
The Rights of Women merit some attention.
First, in the sexes' intermix'd connexion,
One sacred Right of Woman is Protection;
The tender flower that lifts its head elate,
Helpless must fall before the blasts of Fate,
Sunk on the earth, defac'd its lovely form,
Unless your shelter ward th'impending storm.
Our Second Right – but needless here, is caution –
To keep that right inviolate's the fashion;
Each man of sense has it so full before him,
He'd die before he'd wrong it – 'tis Decorum!
There was indeed, in far less polish'd days,
A time when rough, rude Man had naughty ways;
Would swagger, swear, get drunk, kick up a riot,
Nay, even thus, invade a lady's quiet!
Now, thank our stars! those Gothic times are fled;
Now, well-bred men – and you are all well-bred –
Most justly think (and we are much the gainers)
Such conduct, neither spirit, wit nor manners.
For Right the Third – our last, our best, our dearest;

That right to fluttering female hearts the nearest,
Which even the Rights of Kings, in low prostration,
Most humbly own – 'tis dear, dear Admiration!
In that blest sphere alone we live and move;
There, taste that life of life – Immortal Love.
Smiles, glances, fits, fears, flirtations, airs –
'Gainst such a host, what flinty savage dares?
When awful Beauty joins with all her charms,
Who is so rash as rise in rebel arms?
But truce with kings, and truce with constitutions,
With bloody armaments and revolutions;
Let Majesty, your first attention summon
Ah! Ca Ira! The Majesty of Woman!

Rights of Women was openly mirrored on Tom Paine's *Rights of Man*, and was delivered by Louisa as part of an after-piece to Wycherley's *Country Girl* in which she was playing that night. Paine, a fellow exciseman, had to flee to France after publishing his Republican pamphlet in March 1791, and Burns was on dangerous ground in even parodying it as it was held to be treasonable. Copies were circulated covertly and resulted in the formation of the Friends of the People movement. Burns, of course, was in complete sympathy with their aims and with the ideals of the French Revolution but it wasn't a thing normally trumpeted to the world from the stage.

The full repercussions of this were not to be felt by him until later. Meantime, he continued his habit of checking with Mrs Dunlop, and on 6 December sent her a copy, taking advantage, as he said, of the 'double postage'. In another letter to her, towards the end of 1792, he made mention of Thomson's Dramas, but in the same letter went on:

> In our theatre here, *God Save the King* has been met with some groans and hisses, while *Ca Ira* has been repeatedly called for...I sat with my hat on and my arms folded...What my private sentiments are, you will find without an interpreter.

If the times were troubled in Europe, they were no less so for him. Although for the French he shed no tears for Louis and Marie Antoinette on the scaffold.

For Lords and Kings I dinna mourn,
E'en let them die, for that they're born!

Even knowing his responsibilities as a man with a family, he could never quite bridle his tongue, although he tried his best.

Wha will not sing God Save the King,
Shall hang as high's the steeple!
But while we sing God Save the King,
Let's not forget the people!

He was hauled before the Excise Board to answer for his political conduct, but he was, by now, adept at getting himself out of tight corners. He knew exactly whose ear to find, and between October 1792 and January 1793 he wrote lengthily and effectively to the top man, his old admirer and fellow-Jacobite, Robert Graham of Fintry. A brief excerpt from the correspondence admits:

I was in the playhouse one night when Ca Ira was called for. I was in the middle of the pit, and from the pit the clamour arose. One or two individuals with whom I occasionally associate were of the party, but I neither knew of a plot, nor joined a plot, nor ever opened my lips to hiss, or huzza that, or any other political tune whatever. I looked on myself as far too obscure a man to have any weight in quelling a riot.

What he does not say, however, was that he was quite weighty enough to start one. Charles Kirkpatrick Sharpe, an 11-year old at the time, was with his mother at the theatre that night and remembers events differently.

We were at the play in Dumfries in October 1792 – the Caledonian Hunt then being in town. The play was As You Like It, Miss Fontanelle as Rosalind. When God Save the King was called for and sung, we all stood up and uncovered, but Burns sat still in the middle of the pit with his hat on his head. There was a great tumult, with shouts of 'Turn him out!' and 'Shame, Burns!' which continued a good while. At last, he was either expelled or forced to take off his hat – I forgot which, nor can my mother remember. This silly conduct all sensible persons condemned.

Burns, nonetheless, in his letters to Fintry answered every point of criticism with the precision of a lawyer. The Board did not know what to do with him. They could not make him a scapegoat, they dare not make him a martyr, so he was officially reprimanded and returned to his duties. His now overdue promotion was further delayed and he was made to realize how fragile the status of a placeman in Government employ really was. At a time when his talents cried out for a long-overdue place on the Civil List, he was virtually placed under house arrest in the Wee Vennel. What is again ironic is that his troubles came upon him in a theatre.

His fame had by now turned to something resembling notoriety, but not even this, or his theatre-going, stopped him in his avid search for Scottish songs. The *fourth* volume of Johnson's *Musical Museum* had been published in August 1792 and Burns, who had done most of the work on it, also supplied the Preface:

> When the Editor published the third volume of this work, he had reason to conclude that one volume more would finish the publication – Still, however, he has a considerable number of Scots Airs and Songs more than his plan allowed him to include in this fourth volume...These – he shall yet give to the world; that the Scots Musical Museum may be a Collection of every Scots Song extant...

This was an amazing aim, and what is extraordinary is how near Johnson and Burns came to achieving it. On top of this, Alexander Cunningham successfully nominated him for membership of the Royal Archers of Scotland, the Sovereign's ceremonial bodyguard. This was one in the eye for his Dumfries critics. Then, to top it all, publisher Creech suddenly re-appeared on the Burns scene.

Creech wanted to bring out yet another edition, and would Burns be kind enough to supply a further *fifty* pages for it. No wonder Burns could write to Cunningham:

> Amid all my hurry of business, grinding the faces of the Publican & the Sinner on the merciless wheels of the Excise; making ballads, & then drinking, & singing them over; & over & above all, correcting the Presswork of two different publications.

Burns delivered the extra pages, and the edition was published by February 1793. Burns had to ask for some copies for himself – 'to present them among a few Great Folks whom I respect, & a few Little Folks whom I love'. He eventually got 20 presentation copies. Among the Great Folks who received a copy was Maria Riddell, and among the Little Folks was a 12-year old girl at Mossgiel, Elizabeth, his daughter by Bess Paton. It was inscribed – *'her father's gift – THE AUTHOR.'* Robert Burns was always capable of the nice touch when he chose.

His next project came to him similarly out of the blue, and once again it was due to his Edinburgh friend, Alexander Cunningham. Cunningham had recently met with an Edinburgh Civil Servant George Thomson whose hobby was marrying Scots songs to arrangements by leading composers of the day. He engaged composers like Haydn and Beethoven for this task, but Thomson much preferred Haydn's pupil, Pleyel, who was in fashion at that time. The idea of matching the old songs to 'modern' arrangements had been suggested to Thomson by Pietro Urbani, whose Italianate renderings of the old melodies appealed to him. He then considered issuing a volume of these arrangements, and during 1792 had done so with Andrew Erskine, younger brother of the Earl of Kellie (also a composer), who worked with Thomson in 'tidying up' some of the lyrics involved. Unfortunately, young Erskine ran up some heavy gambling debts and threw himself into the Forth, so Thomson was suddenly without a writer. Cunningham suggested Burns.

> To render this work perfect, we are desirous of having the poetry improved, wherever it seems unworthy of the music...some charming melodies are united to mere nonsense and doggerel, while others are accommodated to rhymes so loose and indelicate as cannot be sung in decent company. To remove this reproach would be an easy task to the author of The Cotter's Saturday Night. We shall esteem your poetical assistance a particular favour, besides paying any reasonable price you shall be pleased to demand for it...

It was this last point that raised Burns's anger. He was happy enough to work on any songs, as long as he wasn't hurried in the business, and would indeed submit to Thomson's editorial right (this was an error as it proved) but he would be damned if he would be paid for it.

> As to renumeration, you may think my songs either above or below price; for they shall be absolutely one or the other. In the honest enthusiasm with which I embark in your undertaking, to talk of money, wages, fee, hire, &c, would be downright Sodomy of the Soul!...

This may seem at first sight professionally naive of Burns but it was his true reaction. I have never known an artist of any kind who wasn't first concerned about the fee. Not because that artist was mercenary but because that was the only way he could continue in his art – he had to be paid for it. Many, of course, have other work or private incomes, but for the ordinary freelance artist, the money comes before the inspiration. Burns, however, though employed, had little money to spare to indulge what he called his 'hobbyhorse' of writing. Every shilling he earned was spoken for. Nevertheless, he had his own views about Scottish songs. To him they were as native as a wayside flower, and as available to all. To make a personal profit from what was, for him, a national resource was anathema. This wasn't only high altruism, it was honestly how he saw it. A song was as material as a sunbeam – or a rainbow. What right had he to sell it? It may also have been that Burns had been so irritated and abused by his contractual dealings with Creech, that he wanted nothing to do with any further fiscal dealing in relation to his intellectual property. This again was a mistake, for a proper contract with Thomson would have earned the poet a considerable amount of money. But he was adamant. All he wanted from the enterprise, he told Thomson, was a printed copy of each song he submitted – 'A proof of each of the songs I compose or amend, I shall receive as a favour'.

Thomson was taken aback but was happy to accept his point of view and Burns received his proofs. When he sent Thomson the first batch of songs, half-a-dozen in all, it included classics like *The Lea Rig* and *Duncan Gray*, the tune of which, it is said, he took down from the whistling of a Glasgow carter. It is not generally known how adept Burns had made himself in the practice of musical notation of this kind. By the time that the first part of George Thomson's *Select Airs* had come out in June 1793, Burns had contributed 25 songs as required. That he did this at the same time as carrying out all his other duties is remarkable. But then, we are dealing with a remarkable man. Thomson was delighted, so much so that despite Burns's protestations, he sent the lyricist a five pound note. Burns made the usual high-decibel protests but he kept the money. It could not have come at a better time. He had only recently moved his family out of the overcrowded three rooms in the Wee Vennel into a proper house up the Mill Hole Brae. This move, supervised mainly by Jean, called for extra expense and no doubt the fiver was put to good use.

A more pressing problem was that Britain was now at war with France, which meant that his perks from French imports were no more, and much more dangerously, his pro-French sympathies could now be construed by 'certain persons' as treasonable. It was then that his former neighbour, John Syme, the solicitor, was to prove a good and loyal friend. A few years older than Burns, he had come to Dumfries from Kircudbrightshire to take up the sinecure of Distributor of Stamps for Dumfries in 1791. It will be remembered that when Burns came to Dumfries at the end of the same year, Syme's office was on the floor beneath him. The two became immediate friends and Burns was often a guest at Syme's house in the town. He wrote of Syme –

Who is proof to thy personal converse and wit
Is proof to all other temptation.

Syme found a kindred spirit in Burns. They shared the same love of good talk round a dinner-table as long as the bottle was passed and the talk was of the great events on the other side of the Atlantic and the other side of the Channel. Their sympathies were entirely Republican, but it was a Scottish republicanism, not an American or French one. They were entirely with the theory and the principle of the business, but direct action was out of the question as matters stood. Nevertheless, their open talk got them talked about and this, in itself, could be dangerous. Syme thought that while the poet still had some money in his pocket, it was a good time to get him away from Dumfries. Both were now under the constant watchful eye of authority because of their continued enthusiasm for Revolution and Reform and it would do neither any harm to be out of sight for a time. John Syme made all the arrangements and the only problem was to find a horse for Burns. He no longer kept one as his work was now mostly on foot around the harbour area, so 'Stamp Office Johnny', as Burns called Syme, got him a Highland sheltie for a journey he proposed they make into the area around Galloway. It was decided that the two of them would make a holiday through that part of the country in the last two weeks of July.

CHAPTER 9

First Galloway Tour

(27 July to 2 August 1793)

Dumfries – Parton – Airds – Kenmure – Gatehouse
– Kirkudbright – St Mary's Isle – Wigtown – Daljarrock
– Kirkoswald – Girvan – Lauriston – Dumfries

In wood and wild, ye warbling throng...

Kenmure

THE FRIENDS SET OUT FROM Dumfries on 27 July and went by way of Parton (A29) and Airds (A30) to their first overnight stay at Kenmure Castle (A31). Here they stayed with the Gordons, and one of the first things Burns did was to make an epitaph at Mrs Gordon's request on her pet dog, Elcho, which had just died. It was not one of his most memorable efforts.

This visit was only notable for the fact that he ruined a new pair of riding boots carrying an elderly minister on his back to shore when their rowing boat, taking guests on a sail down the loch, grounded in the shallows. It was a gallant gesture by Burns to allow himself to be so 'priest-ridden', but the act cost him his brand-new boots, or rather, their inexpert drying made them unfit to wear. Burns wasn't too pleased. The boots had cost him half a week's wages.

Selkirk

Syme described him as being in 'a most epigrammatic mood' on the journey next day to St Mary's Isle (A34) where they were to be the guests of the Earl of Selkirk. Syme's exact word was *accable* to describe the combination of headache and stomach-ache that made the poet 'without boots...fume and rage' against the Earl of

Galloway, the local High Tory, whose house they passed as they rode along. When the noble lord heard of Burns's disparaging remarks, he said he 'could not feel hurt by the attacks of a licentious, rhyming ploughman'. It is the only thing his Lordship is remembered for today. Burns's mood wasn't much better when they eventually reached Selkirk's seat that night, where among the guests was no less than Signor Urbani. Songs were sung and discussed and the talk went round with the wine. No doubt this helped Burns to regain his usual social composure.

Some hae meat and canna eat
And some wad eat that want it
But we hae meat and we can eat
And sae the Lord be thankit.

This grace before meals, now termed the Selkirk Grace, was supposedly delivered for the first time at this same meal, but Syme doesn't mention it. Burns could have delivered a grace *extempore* on that occasion as it was his custom to do so when a guest. And he might also have done so next evening at the Old Heid Inn, now called the Selkirk Arms, where a plaque on the wall boasts the fact that he did. There was indeed an old Galloway Grace which Burns might have adapted, but what has survived in every Burns edition ever since is the now-accepted version. If it is his reworking on the spot of a very ancient Scottish fragment, it illustrates again his genius for on-the-spot recreation. Later in the evening Burns recited his own *Lord Gregory* 'to a stunned reaction' as John Syme reported:

Twas such a silence as a mind of feeling must necessarily preserve when it is touched, as I sometimes think will happen, with that sacred enthusiasm which banishes every other thought that the contemplation and indulgence of the sympathy produced...

This is the kind of silence actors recognise as the very height of applause.

Burns must have been on form that night at Lord Selkirk's table. Syme, at any rate, called it 'a most happy evening'. The following morning, Selkirk himself took the poet's boots for repair in

Dumfries. His Lordship was not a typical Lord. He was a radical and shared the egalitarian views of men like the lawyer, Thomas Muir of Huntershill, who were hounded for their liberal views. Selkirk was indeed a 'Friend of the People' and his welcome to Burns was all the warmer for sharing the same views. Syme was delighted with the occasion – 'the poet acquitted himself to admiration. The lion that had raged so heavily in the morning was now as mild and gentle as a lamb. Next day, we returned to Dumfries and so ended our peregrination.' No doubt Burns got his boots back as good as new, but the real value of the trip was that Burns returned with a classic song in his saddle bag. Whether it was the result of his 'lion's raging' of the morning's ride, or just another outcome of his mercurial moodiness Syme had noticed on the trip, we shall never know, but a patriotic something came to the boil on that ride and burst into life as a famous song.

It had been more than five years since he had first seen the field of Bannockburn (A44), but the germ of the idea had lain in his brain since then and it emerged through the hangover that morning in August 1793 with astounding fervour. It can still sound a clarion today:

Scots wha hae wi' Wallace bled,
Scots wham Bruce has aften led,
Welcome to your gory bed
Or to victorie.

Signor Urbani may also have played his part in the genesis. It was he who suggested that Burns write 'soft verses' for the tune that Thomas Fraser, the bandmaster, had played to Burns on his hautboy [oboe] recently in Dumfries. Urbani and Burns may have talked about this air, especially as it was said to be Bruce's march to Bannockburn. They were hardly 'soft verses' Burns gave to this martial tune, but Urbani's English was perhaps not as good as his singing. The fact remains that a song was born on this Galloway tour and everyone concerned is remembered by it.

Burns was tempted to a more overt political stance, but the sight of poor Muir being taken in chains from Stranraer to Edinburgh to stand trial for possessing Tom Paine's *Rights of Man* was a warning to Burns's more temperate friends, who made him hide his own copy with a neighbour. He was encouraged to put his mind to other things like his songs – or even to the theatre. His verses here could properly be described as 'soft'. He dashed off *On Seeing Miss Fontanelle in a Favourite Character* less than a year after her delivery of his controversial Address for her, but this was little more than an epigram:

Sweet naivete of feature
Simple, wild, enchanting elf,
Not to thee, but thanks to Nature,
Thou art acting but thyself.
Wert thou awkward, stiff, affected,
Spurning Nature, scorning Art,
Loves and Graces all rejected
Then indeed, thou'd'st act a part!

He followed this with a somewhat overblown, over-written letter to her on 1 December containing another Address ('May it be a Prologue to an overflowing house...') for her Benefit performance at the Theatre Royal three days later.

Address Spoken by Miss Fontanelle on her Benefit at the Theatre, Dumfries:

Still anxious to secure your partial favor,
And no less anxious, sure, this night than ever,
A Prologue, Epilogue, or some such matter,
'Twould vamp my bill, said I, if nothing better:
So sought a Poet roosted near the skies;
Told him I came to feast my curious eyes;
Said, nothing like his works was ever printed;
And last, my prologue-business slily hinted.
'Ma'am, let me tell you,' quoth my man of rhymes,
'I know your bent – these are no laughing times:
Can you – but, Miss, I own my fears –
Dissolve in pause, and sentimental tears?
With laden sighs, and solemn-rounded sentence,
Rouse from his sluggish slumbers, fell repentance?

Paint Vengeance as he takes his horrid stand,
Waving on high the desolating brand,
Calling the storms to bear him o'er a guilty land?'
I could do more! Askance, the creature eyeing:-
'D'ye think,' said I, 'this face wade for crying?
I'll laugh, that's poz – nay more, the world shall know it;
And so, your servant, gloomy Master Poet!'
Firm as my creed, Sirs, 'tis my fix'd belief
That Misery's another word for Grief.
I also think (so may I be a bride!)
That so much laughter, so much life enjoyed.
Thou man of crazy care and ceaseless sigh,
Still under bleak Misfortune's blasting eye;
Doom'ed to that sorest task of man alive-
To make three guineas do the work of five;
Laugh in Misfortune's face – the beldam witch-
Say, you'll be merry tho' you can't be rich!
Thou other man of care, the wretch in love!
Who, long with jiltish arts and airs has strove;
Who, as the bows all temptingly project,
Measur'st in desperate thought - a rope - thy neck-
Or, where the beetling cliff o'erhangs the deep,
Peerest to meditate the healing leap:
Would'st thou be cured, thou silly, moping elf?
Laugh at her follies - laugh e'en at thyself;
Learn to despise those frowns now so terrific,
And love a kinder; that's your grand specific.
To sum up all: be merry, I advise;
And as we're merry, may we still be wise.

What is interesting in this is Burns's attempt at a self-mocking, if heavy-handed, dialogue element within a normally declamatory form. But he was in low spirits at the time. Fontanelle came to him in his new house ('a Poet roosted near the skies') in the upstairs room where he had his books and his writing-table, to ask him to write the piece. What would have served best for both of them would have been his going to her at the theatre. The effect of seeing actors at work in rehearsal, in the atmosphere of greasepaint and painted scenery, surrounded by stage costumes and properties, might have aroused any latent theatrical instinct in him – and also given him a much-needed practical introduction to its methods. The players themselves would have taught him how to write a play if indeed there was a play in him. Only involved activity at close quarters would have got it out of him. Unfortunately, the opportunity was missed and was never to come again.

Dr Mackay, like many distinguished Burns critics, laments the fact that Burns never took time in Dumfries to edit a volume of his own songs. Burns had often expressed a desire to do this, if only to protect himself from the rubbish that was printed and sold in his name on the streets. Ballad-making was always his 'hobby-horse' despite how much he took it seriously, but it is to be regretted that he never did get round to it. (I feel the same way with regard to a Burns play – despite having 'serious thoughts' on the possibility.) However, he still enjoyed seeing plays and continued to attend the Theatre Royal as a guest of the management. The Riddell family had a box and Burns often attended in their company – or more particularly, in that of Maria Riddell.

> I meant to have called on you yesternight (at the theatre) but as I edged up to your box, the first object that greeted my view was one of those lobster-coated puppies, sitting, like another dragon, guarding the Hesperion fruit...

It was one of Maria's many young army officer admirers. Burns beat a strategic retreat.

He made other advances on his elegant new pen-friend and was not always repulsed. The personal magnetism that had enthralled the Edinburgh ladies still had its echo in Dumfries. Miss Dorothea Benson attended a ball given by the Caledonian Hunt in the Assembly Rooms. She was on the dance-floor with a young officer when Burns entered.

> An immediate whisper went round the room – 'There's Burns!' I looked round and there he was. His bright dark eyes fell upon me. I shall never forget that look. It was one that gave me no pleasure...

However, young ladies are often thrilled by what they subconsciously fear. She needn't have worried because, as she went on, 'He soon left the meeting'.

Between the thick-headed officer class and the small-minded petty bourgeoisie, Burns found himself in an uncomfortable pincer during his Dumfries days. When he might have been at his writing desk, he was out on his rounds. So many lesser writers were favoured by sinecures of one kind or another, Burns had none. He had the ear of so many of the great in distant places, yet he could not win the nod from those supposed superiors right at his elbow. That was to be a large cause of his troubles. He was often called on to make toasts at public dinners, a dangerous exercise in his hands. For instance, 'Here's to the last verse of the last chapter of the last Book of Kings!' This reads – Ch25 v30 – *And he appointed him a continual allowance given him of the king, day by day, all the days of his life.* This seems a very reasonable appeal by a servant of King George for a place on the Civil List to which his poetic status entitled him one would think – yet it offended some. When asked to propose a toast to the Prime Minister, he offered it as – *'To a better man, George Washington'.* A lesser man might have been arrested immediately, but such was his presence, and his fame, he went untouched, although it was a near thing on occasions.

What added to his concerns was a continued fondness for the convivial hour and the challenge of the *bon mot*, despite his inability, both financial and constitutional, to keep up the general required pace of consumption.

> There are gentlemen here in Dumfries, five bottle a night men, who would not give me their company if I did not drink with them - so I give to each, a slice of my constitution...

This was so sadly true and it began to tell more and more as time went by.

The truth was, Dumfries didn't know what to do with Burns. Had he conformed, he might have been safely accepted and even assisted, but he almost went out of his way to be awkward at times, particularly when he 'had drink taken' as they say. The other gentlemen were often more drunk than he but they kept it private. Burns went public with everything – his thoughts, his feelings, his loves, and it all came out when he had a glass in his hand and company at his elbow. He could never resist an audience, but he had neither the head nor the stomach for drink. With him, a very little went a long way. He would be well aware that when 'guid drink gaes in, guid sense gaes oot'.

> Hard drinking is the devil to me. Against this I have again & again bent my resolution, & have greatly succeeded. Taverns, I have totally abandoned: it is the private parties in the family way, among the hard-drinking gentlemen of this country that does me the mischief...

The party in this case was at Friars' Carse, the home of the Riddell family, on a cold December night in 1793. While the ladies retired to the drawing-room, the men passed the port around in the dining-room encouraging Burns to 'perform' – and to drink. The talk got round to the Roman myth of the Rape of the Sabine Women and some of the army officers present thought it would be fun to re-enact the scene – not seriously, of course, but to give the ladies a little, pleasurable scare. Each man present was allotted a lady in the company as his particular 'victim' and Burns was assigned Maria Riddell – already attracted to him, and an admirer. It was then he who, as 'the leading Roman of them all', led the 'attack' on the drawing room of 'Sabines'. One can imagine their startled reaction. One can also imagine Burns's horror when, as he seized Maria as planned, he was the only man in the room. It had all been a conspiracy by the young army men to take their revenge on Burns for dominating the table and fascinating the ladies. Burns, of course, was ignominiously ordered to leave the house by the older Mrs Riddell. Some of the ladies, seeing through the ploy, tried to speak up for Burns, but now the men entered and purported to be shocked at the animal behaviour of a common gauger. Burns was totally humiliated – and could say nothing. Sobered by how he had been so crassly duped, he rode home, ashamed of himself yet enraged by such calculated 'play-acting' on the part of his fellow guests.

The next morning, despite a dreadful hangover, he wrote to his hostess, Elizabeth Riddell, an hysterical letter of apology – 'from the regions of Hell, amid the horrors of the damned', but he added – 'to the men of the company I will make no apology – (they) were partakers of my guilt...But to you, Madam, I have much to apologise...' He received no acknowledgment. He had drunk too much, he knew, but so had the other men. Once again, it was a piece of misjudged theatricality which had been his undoing. Maria Riddell refused to speak to him when they met later in a Dumfries street and chose not to answer his many letters. Burns was never to recover his social status after this tragic charade. He took his poetic revenge on her in his *From Esopus to Maria*. It should be noted that Esopus was a Roman actor at the time of Cicero.

> *From these drear scenes my wretched lines I date*
> *To tell Maria her Esopus' fate.*
> *'Alas! I feel I am no actor here!'*
> *Tis real hangmen real scourges bear!*
> *Prepare, Maria, for a horrid tale...*
> *The hero of the mimic scene no more,*
> *I start in Hamlet, in Othello roar;*
> *Or, haughty Chieftain, 'mid the din of arms,*
> *In Highland bonnet woo Malvina's charms:*
> *While sans-culottes stoop up the mountain high,*
> *And steal me from Maria's prying eye...*
> *The shrinking bard adown the alley skulks,*
> *And dreads a meeting worse that Woolwich hulks,*
> *Though there, his heresies in Church and State*
> *Might well award him Muir and Palmer's fate...*
> *Maria, send me too thy griefs and cares,*
> *In all of thee sure thy Esopus shares...*
> *For who can write and speak as thou and I...?*

'Esopus' conceals the identity of Williamson, the former manager of the Dumfries company of players, who had also been part of the Riddell circle and was imprisoned at one time as a vagrant, merely because he was an actor. Burns felt something of the same sense of being outlawed by the Riddells, and he used this long satire to hit back. A sad rider to a gloomy year was that the poet's only living daughter by Jean, born in the previous year, had been named Elizabeth Riddell Burns.

He could not remain long away from controversy. In January 1794, at a dinner held in the King's Arms, he gave the company another controversial toast – '*May our success in the present war [against France] be equal to the justice of our cause!*' Not the sort of remark to win friends among the politicians or the military, especially with a certain Captain Dodd of Chapel, who though it sufficient to warrant a duel. Burns had to think fast with his pen. Once again his wit had got him in trouble and, once again, it must get him out. He might well have faced up to the angry Captain, for he was man enough and had his own brace of pistols, but he knew that would not be the clever thing to do. He wrote quickly to the Clerk of the Peace, Samuel Clark –

> I was, I know, drunk last night, but I am sober this morning...the words were such as generally I believe end in pistols, but I am still pleased to think I did not ruin the peace...Farther, you know that the report of certain Political opinions being mine has already once before brought me to the brink of destruction – I dread last night's business may be represented in the same way – YOU, I beg, will take care to prevent it...

Mr Clerk (of the Peace) lived up to his title and the matter was smoothed over. Burns knew his own failings, but he also knew he wasn't as bad as he was painted.

> Some of our folks...had & perhaps still have conceived a prejudice against me as being a drunken, dissipated character – I might be all this, and still be an honest fellow...

In 1792 Burns had been Senior Warden of the St Andrew's Lodge of Dumfries, but latterly he had almost ceased to attend Masonic meetings. However, he was there on 6 May 1794 when David McCulloch was admitted a member. McCulloch had been in Paris at the fall of the Bastille and spoke fluent French. He returned to Dumfries on the death of his father, and he and Burns became friends almost at once. What drew them together was not only their love of France and all things French, but a greater love and enthusiasm for Scottish songs. McCulloch had a fine tenor voice and assisted Burns from time to time in singing over new lyrics as they came from his pen. A confirmed bachelor, McCulloch never married, and after Burns's death went off to India to become a merchant there. This affable young man came from the neighbourhood of Ardwall, close to Gatehouse (A32), and asked the Bard to visit him if he were ever in that area. Burns promised he would get in touch, and he did.

> My long projected journey through your country is at last fixed, & on Wednesday next, if you have nothing of more importance than to take a saunter down to Gatehouse, about two or three o'clock, I shall be happy to take a draught of Mckune's best with you...Syme goes also to Kirroughtree, & let me remind you to accompany me there, – I will need all the friends I can muster, for I am indeed ill at ease whenever I approach our Honourables and Right Honourables.

He was gradually realising that on any social occasion now he was in need of 'minders', friends that might stand by him in any situation to hold him back – or hold him up. Syme arranged that they leave Dumfries on 25 June.

CHAPTER 10

Second Galloway Tour

(25 to 28 June 1794)

Dumfries – Castle Douglas – Gatehouse – Newton Stewart
– Kirroughtree – Portpatrick – Dumfries.

SYME HAD GONE AHEAD on Stamp business so Burns was left on his own at the Carlinwark Inn, Castle Douglas (A38). He was never very good on his own. He thrived on company but that night there was none to be had – except a bottle of wine. 'Here am I set, a solitary hermit, in the solitary room of a solitary inn, with a solitary bottle of wine by me.' He spent the time writing a long, nostalgic letter to Nancy McLehose – 'Clarinda? What a host of Memory's tenderest offspring crowd on my fancy at that sound!' Writing letters always seemed to make him feel better.

> You must know, my dearest Madam, that these now many years, wherever I am, in whatever company, when a married lady is called as toast, I constantly give YOU; but as your name has never passed my lips, even to my most intimate friend, I give you by the name of Mrs Mac. This is so well known among my acquaintants, that when my married lady is called for, the toast-master will say – 'O, we need not ask him who it is – here's Mrs Mac!'...I devote this glass of wine to a most ardent wish for your happiness!

No doubt the bottle was drunk that night.

The next day he went on to Kirroughtree (A40) with Syme and from there to 'drink tea' with Jean Lorimer and her family. Jean was Burns's 'Chloris', the *'Lass wi' the Lint-White Locks'* and much sought-after by at least three of his younger fellow-officers in the Excise, but she denied them all and married a local farmer (who deserted her three years later to escape his creditors). Jean, however, always remained a favourite with Burns and the Burns family, and was the heroine of many of Burns's songs at this period. One of them was written on behalf of one particular suitor, John Gillespie, who was later transferred from Dumfries to Portpatrick (A41), where Burns spent his last day of this brief break before returning to Dumfries. He had really only given company to Syme while he was on business, but Burns never said no to a trip. It was his last holiday jaunt.

Poor Jean was never to have much luck. Her father went senile and she had to fend for herself and eventually made her way, via various positions, to Craigieburn, in Moffat (A26). James Hogg, the Ettrick Shepherd, who met her in Edinburgh much later, said that she had told him that she and Burns had made love every time he visited Moffat, but there is no evidence of this other than her word, and his more than twenty songs about her, the best-known perhaps being *I'll Ay Ca' in by Yon Toon* with its next line – 'to see my bonnie Jean again', meaning Jean Lorimer. Burns himsef wrote to Thomson, 'I assure you that to my lovely friend you are indebted for many of your best songs of mine' – more than any other of the charmers, even his own Jean. It also helped that Jean Lorimer, like Jean Armour, was a beautiful and natural singer. She is the least known of the Burns heroines, yet Dr James Adams wrote a whole book about her in 1901. The doctor's father was Jean's doctor while she lived in Edinburgh as 'Mrs Lorimer' and he said that Burns also knew her Edinburgh. However, the best testimonial to their true relationship might be the book of his poems that he presented to her on 3 August 1795, and in which he had written –

> Inscription, written on the blank leaf of a copy of the last edition of my poems, presented to the lady whom, in so many fictitious reveries of passion, but with the most ardent sentiments of real friendship, I have so often sung under the name of 'Chloris'.

I think we can leave it at that.

On return to Dumfries, and even with the war with France still in progress, Burns set to work to restore his good name in the Excise after the various frights he had been given in the recent turbulent times. What he was really after was the promotion which his unthinking outbursts had prevented, and he knew he would have to regularise his position very soon if the job was ever to give him the security he knew he would need as he got older. Of course, as has been said, he could have eased his worries almost at once by entering into a normal contractual relationship with George Thomson about royalties for the songs, but he was still adamant that he would never sell a song.

As usual, whenever he wanted a favour, in any area, he started at the top. In January 1794, he opened his campaign for advancement by writing to Graham of Fintry suggesting, no less, the total restructuring of the Dumfries Excise Division:

> What I have long digested, & am going to propose, is the reduction of one of our Dumfries Divisions. – Not only in these unlucky times, but even in the highest flush of business, my Division, though by far the heaviest, was mere trifling – the others were likely still less. I would plan the reduction as thus – Let the second Division be annihilated; and be divided among the others...

He then follows with a lot of impressive technical detail, which only serves to further highlight what a good Excise Officer he would have made had he applied himself less to song-writing and other pleasant pursuits like touring and country dinners. What he was suggesting to his superiors was no less than cost-cutting efficiencies, which any modern time-and-motion expert might have considered advisable in similar circumstances. Burns goes on –

> I assure you, Sir, that, by my plan, the Duties will be equally well charged, & thus an Officer's appointment saved to the Public.- You must remark one thing; that our Common Brewers are, every man of them in Dumfries, completely & unexceptionably, Fair Traders. – One, or two, rascally creatures are in the Bridgend Division, but besides being nearly ruined, as all Smugglers deserve, by fines & forfeitures, their business is on the most trifling scale you can fancy – I must beg of you, Sir, should my plan please you, that you will conceal my hand in it, & give it as your own thought. – My warm & worthy friend, Mr Corbet, may think me an impertinent inter-meddler in his department; & Mr Findlater, my Supervisor, who is not only one of the first, if not the very

> first of Excisemen in your Service, but is also one of the worthiest fellows in the universe; he, I know, would feel hurt at it; & as he is one of my most intimate friends, you can easily figure how it would place me, to have my plan known to be mine. – For farther information on the Subject, permit me to refer you to a young beginner whom you lately sent among us, Mr Andrew Pearson; a gentleman I am happy to say, from manner, abilities & attention, promises to be indeed a great acquisition to the service of your Honorable Board.

The fact that one poor exciseman would lose his job in this re-arrangement didn't seem to bother Burns, but Fintry saw the real reason behind Burns's letter and nothing was done about his proposals. Nothing daunted, a month later, he wrote again. This time, it was to baldly ask for promotion.

> The language of supplication is almost the only language in which I have it in my power to approach you; & I have your generous commands for coming to you with it, on every opportunity...

He certainly did, and on this occasion he did so because he had heard that certain promotions at a high level were impending. He offered himself as the replacement in Dumfries were these moves to take place. How he came to know this is only a further instance of the extent of his network. As it happened, the moves were made and Burns was marked for the post he applied for – but by that time, he had been a year dead.

It is not a pretty side of our poet, this drive for self-preservation, but it only shows how desperate he had become to stabilise his finances. Yet, had he said nothing, he was already earmarked for promotion, but somehow his high-placed friends had failed to tell him that, and so we have the unseemly sight of one of the best minds in Scotland scrabbling for what were really puny posts. When Findlator, the Supervisor at Dumfries, fell ill, Burns took his place with no problem whatsoever as Acting Supervisor.

Then, quite suddenly, an offer came from the *Morning Chronicle* in London. James Perry, an Aberdeen man, had become editor and proprietor, and offered Burns a guinea a week for a weekly poem. This was more than he could earn in the Excise, and would possibly be a day's work at the most, yet, inexplicably,

Burns turned down the offer – 'Your offer is indeed truly generous, & most sincerely, I thank you for it; but in my present situation, I find I dare not accept it...' Why not? It could only be that he had decided to put all his eggs in the Excise basket with the song-work for Thomson as his continuing 'hobby-horse'. He must have thought he had the Supervisorship at Dumfries in his pocket. He had, but what he didn't know was that time itself would finally catch him out. Or perhaps he did know. Hence his untypical grovelling and haste for security for Jean and the children.

Who is to know with genius? As if to emphasise his anxieties, another son, James Glencairn Burns, was born on 12 August 1794 – making it six children under his wing. Little wonder he found it harder to fly than he once did.

On the other hand, he is seen here as being more in command of himself – 'my political sins seem to have been forgiven me' – and what was even better for the other side of his nature, he was reconciled to Maria Riddell. She sent a book to him and he acknowledged it. It was little more than a formal exchange, but at least the barriers were down and they could resume *almost* as they were the year before. In the New Year of 1795, Burns wrote to Mrs Dunlop –

> What a transient business is life! Very lately, I was a boy; but t'other day I was a young man; & already I begin to feel the rigid fibre & stiffening joints of Old Age coming fast o'er my frame.

While this may be fanciful – after all, he was only 35 – it did indicate his increasing worry about his health. He had always been something of a valetudinarian, with some justification it may be added, but now it was to be more of an obsession. Not that it stopped him writing with all his old verve and fire. The year began in a blaze with *A Man's A Man*. This hymn to equality was sent off to Thomson almost simultaneously with the letter to Mrs Dunlop. This was the real Burns speaking. He had been told officially that he was a place-man, and must know his place. He had been reminded that he was not a gentleman, that he was of the plebeian class, but his Bible reading had acquainted him with Hasidic prayer – 'Grant us, O Lord, we may never forget that every man and woman is the son and daughter of a king'. Privately, he was to exclaim in his sickness: 'Like Balaak to Balaam – come, curse me, Jacob! Come, defy me, Israel!' And also to admit, like Hamlet, that 'Man delights me not, nor woman neither!' Publicly, however, at the outset of what was to be his penultimate year came a blast that rang out like a trumpet for the rights of the ordinary man.

Like Wordsworth and many other artists and writers in Britain, Burns had been thrilled at first with the assertion of the Republican cause in France, but then, like Wordsworth again, he became somewhat disillusioned by events that followed the French Revolution. Nonetheless, unlike the Englishman, he still held to the ideals of human brotherhood that first inspired both of them. Even at, what seemed to him, the lowest level of his own health and fortune, he delivered these lines to the world from Dumfries, Scotland. They deserve to be written in full, for they have all the best of Burns in them – courage and hope and belief in the essential worth of Man.

> *Is there for honest poverty*
> *That hangs his head an' a' that?*
> *The coward slave we pass him by,*
> *We daur be poor for a' that!*
> *For a' that, an' a' that,*
> *Our toils obscure an' a' that,*
> *The rank is but the guinea-stamp,*
> *The man's the gowd for a' that.*
> *What tho' on hamely fare we dine,*
> *Wear hodden grey, an' a' that,*
> *Gie fules their silks and knaves their wine,*
> *A man's a man for a' that.*
> *For a' that, an' a' that,*
> *Their tinsel show, an' a' that,*
> *The honest man, tho' e'er sae poor,*
> *Is king o' men for a' that.*
> *Ye see yon birkie ca'd a Lord,*
> *Wha struts and stares an' a' that,*
> *Tho' hunners worship at his word,*

He's but a coof, for a' that.
For a' that, an' a' that,
His ribband star, an' a' that,
The man o' independent mind,
He looks an' laughs at a' that.
A prince can make a belted knight,
A marquis, duke, an' a' that,
But an honest man's aboon his might.
Guid faith, he maunna fa' that!
For a' that, an' a' that,
Their dignities, an' a' that,
The pith o' sense, and pride o' worth
Are higher rank than a' that.
Then let us pray that come it may,
As come it will, for a' that,
That sense and worth, o'er a' the earth,
Shall bear the 'gree, an' a' that.
For a' that, an' a' that,
It's comin' yet for a' that,
That man to man, the world o'er,
Shall brothers be, for a' that.

In a nice touch, James Perry published the song in his *Morning Chronicle*. It was the first time that this most Scottish of effusions had appeared in print – and it was in a London journal. For a' that, and a' that, Burns headed no republican revolution in Scotland, nor spearheaded any national revival in either country by virtue of what he said or wrote. Who knows, more than two hundred years on, in the second millennium, his words may be taken up yet by a new Scotland – and a new world. He spoke for all men in every age but he wouldn't be the first man of words to be ahead of his time.

The reality, however, is that he was bound to his time as much as he was to his writing desk. His only sanity was to keep writing as long as he could hold the goosefeather in his hand. *Last May a Braw Wooer* went to the Thomson collection with half a dozen more. *Leezie Lindsay* was a fragment saved for Johnson's

Museum, only one of twenty Burns contributions published in that series from that year. But if the muse were still ablaze, the goose-feather trembled. He was so weakened he even gave up the Masons.

Yet, ludicrous as it may seem, it was at this time, against all his political principles, he joined the Volunteer Militia. That this was also a kind of political gesture to draw the fire of his enemies in the town, there is no doubt, and though there were mutterings of protest, there was no actual opposition to his admission as founder member of the Dumfries section. William Pitt had called on all patriotic citizens to take up arms against a possible French invasion. Burns took up his pen and *Does Haughty Gaul Invasion Threat* was written to pay lip service to the required patriotism. What no one expected was that he would also buy a uniform from David Williamson, the tailor, and line up with the Establishment. One suspects Syme's hand in this. Each volunteer was expected to serve 'during the present war, without pay and find their own clothing'. The uniform was described as 'a blue coat, half-lapelled, with red cape and cuffs, and gilt buttons with RDV engraved, a plain white vest with small gilt buttons, white trousers, white stockings, a black velvet stock and black shoes with black ribbons'. Hats were supplied at 16 shillings each. These were round, turned up at the left side with a gilt button and sporting a black cockade. It was quite an ensemble. Perhaps the dandy in Burns was attracted to the uniform. At any rate, newly-attired (at a considerable cost for Burns) the Volunteers met on 20 February 1795 and elected Colonel de Peyster, a former army man, as their Major Commandant. Private Burns and Private Syme were duly in attendance, and a month later, before drill in the Dock Park, they took the required Oath of Allegiance.

In Burns's phrase, the Dumfries Royal Volunteers were an 'awkward squad', but he surprised them all with his own 'dexterity in handling arms'. Unfortunately, he missed the inaugural march through Dumfries on 26 March, being delayed at home with 'toothache'. It was a timely ailment. The prospect of a public march through the town in this particular company might have been too much for his conscience. Whatever, he was there later to record for posterity – 'This day the Volunteer's drum beat for the first time'. Syme also recorded:

> Burns and I are one and indivisible, but what with his occupation and mine, we meet only by Starts – or at least occasionally – and we drink as many cups of tea as bottles of wine together. We are two of the best privates in the Dumfries Royal Volunteers. But not to flatter myself nor him, I would say that hang me if I should know how to be happy were he not in the way of making me so at time.

It is a manly tribute to both of them.

Because of the war, things were bad for Burns and the Excise with no French imports, but they were also bad for everyone, especially the poor. There was a shortage of bread, for instance, and there were riots in the streets. The gentlemen of the town, however, seemed still able to have their convivial public dinners. Burns's last public act was at one of these and again it was a controversial toast. At the dinner hosted by the Dumfries Royal Volunteers to celebrate Lord Rodney's naval victory over the French, Burns was, as usual, called upon to make the toast, and, as usual, he did not give them what they expected. They rose dutifully as Burns raised his glass, and then as he said, 'Gentlemen, may we never see the French, nor the French see us', it was reported that 'most of the Volunteers dropped to their seats like so many old wives at a field-preaching but not a few raxed their jaws at the homely truth and humour of the poet's sentiments'. It was his final public appearance.

One afternoon shortly afterwards, sometime in May 1795, David McCulloch, the Masonic tenor of the year before, had ridden to Dumfries to attend a ball in the evening in honour of the King's Birthday, and he was –

> very sorry to see Burns walking alone on the shady side of the High Street, while opposite was gay with successive groups of ladies and gentlemen, all drawn together for the festivities of the night, not one of whom appeared willing to recognise him.

McCulloch quickly dismounted and hurried over to Burns, asking why he was not with the crowds on the other side of the street. Burns merely raised a hand and shook his head, saying – 'Nay, nay, my young friend. That's all over now.' He had been invited to the same ball as a guest of Maria Riddell, but declined the invitation. His days of public performance were over and he knew it. As when he was ill in Irvine (A6) in 1781, he began to be preoccupied with thoughts of death, but it was his three-year-old Elizabeth who died, she who had been named for the Riddells. His only comment was – 'autumn robbed me of my daughter', but any father would know how he must have felt losing a child at that age. He began to suffer painfully from his old rheumatic fever. From this point on he was in decline and even his letters show it –

> ...& long the dice spun doubtful; until after many weeks of a sick-bed it seems to have turned up life, & I am beginning to crawl across the room, & once indeed have been before my own door in the street.

It is a sad picture of a man who, not long before, was so full of fame and energy.

> I have great hopes that the approaching summer will set me to rights, but as yet, I cannot boast of returning health. I have now reason to believe that my complaint is a flying gout.

It was Dr William Maxwell who diagnosed Burns's acute endocarditis as 'flying gout', hence his prescription for 'sea-bathing, horse riding and country quarters', the then accepted cure for this condition. Burns's *per annum* had been cut to half so country quarters were out; he had done plenty of horse riding with no great results; so only sea-bathing remained. He was advised to try the Solway Firth and to drink the waters of the Brow Well. For a man in his condition, sea-bathing in the chilly Solway was just about the very worst thing he could have done, but how was he – or Dr Maxwell – to know that? Anyway, Brow (A42) wasn't so far from home and it would be 'convenient', so Burns agreed. How many have similarly died from doctor's guesses?

William Maxwell, however, was recognised as having a high professional skill for his time. He was a year younger than Burns, a Catholic and a Jacobite – a rare combination in Dumfries. One has the feeling he was Burns's doctor out of their shared republican principles rather than medical acumen, but Burns had been drawn to him because Maxwell, who was educated in France, had been in Paris at the time of the French Revolution. It was even said that he had dipped his handkerchief in the blood of Louis and Antoinette at their execution, but many thought this one of the young doctor's stories. So the trip was decided and arrangements made. It was the last throw of the dice by Burns. One last gamble to regain his body.

Before going, however, he worked on his last songs – *O, lay thy loof in mine, lass, Here's a health to ane I lo'e dear*, and the incomparable *O wert thou in the cauld blast*. This was dedicated to the young girl who nursed him in this last illness, Jessie Lewars. She was the daughter of a former Supervisor of the Excise in Dumfries and sister of John Lewars who worked with Burns (and also *for* him when Burns was too ill to go on his rounds). The Lewars family lived opposite the Burns family on the Mill Brae, and Jessie often helped Jean with the children. Now the husband, too, was in her care. Jean was confined in the last stages of pregnancy and could not care for him herself, so Jessie looked after them all. It was for this young girl then that Burns wrote his last great song –

O wert thou in the cauld blast
On yonder lea, on yonder lea,
My plaidie to the angry airt,
I'd shelter thee, I'd shelter thee

He wrote it for her to sing, and she did. He also wrote to James Johnson:

My wife has a very particular friend of hers, a young lady who sings well, to whom she wishes to present the Scots Musical Museum. If you have a spare copy, will you be so obliging as to send it by the very first fly, as I am anxious to have it soon.

The good Johnson sent it by return and Jessie sang every tune in it as he lay there.

James Clarke, the former Moffat schoolmaster, owed Burns money and had been paying it off by instalments. Burns, now on half salary, had to ask him for an extra guinea on the next instalment, saying –

> Alas Clarke, I begin to fear the worst! As to my individual self, I am tranquil – I would despise myself were I not – but for Burns's poor widow, & half a dozen of his dear little ones, helpless orphans, there I am as weak as a woman's tear – Enough of this! It is half my sickness...

His last song was on his table. He finished it with a struggle –

Then come, thou fairest of the fair,
Those wonted smiles, O let me share,
And by thy beauteous self I swear
No love but thine my heart shall know.

Then it was time to take the cart to Brow.

Brow

(3 - 18 July 1796)
Dumfries – Brow – Dumfries

THE HAMLET OF BROW (A42) is on the shores of the Solway only a few miles south of Dumfries. The waters of the well, drunk from a cup chained to its side, were held to contain medicinal properties, but really it was only salt water. It may have had in its saline constituents an iron or chalybeate element but it was only sea water for all that. Still, people thought it did them good, and for that reason it probably did. It can only be concluded that Burns did not react well to it, for after three weeks he was worse if anything. This, of course, might have been the additional practice of a daily immersion in the Solway up to the armpits. Whatever the reason, the cures were worse than the disease. He stayed at the only inn in the place, somewhat rough and ready premises and he was only too glad to escape from the place whenever he could. One of the first outings was to see Maria Riddell. She had come to nearby Lochmaben (A25) for her own health. Hearing that Burns was at Brow, she immediately sent her carriage for him. She wrote later:

I was struck by his appearance on entering the room. The stamp of death was imprinted on his features. He seemed already [to be] touching the brink of eternity. His first salutation was – 'Well, Madam, have you any commands for the other world?' ...We had a long and serious conversation about his present situation...his anxiety for his family seem to hang heavy upon him...He was well aware that his death would occasion some noise and that every scrap of writing would be revived against him to the injury of his future reputation...On this account, he deeply regretted having deferred to put his papers into a state of arrangement, as he was now quite incapable of the exertion...At table he ate little or nothing, but the conversation was kept up with great evenness and animation on his part. I had seldom seen his mind greater or more collected. There was frequently a considerable degree of vivacity in his sallies...We parted about sunset...to meet no more.

Syme also visited and was horrified at the change in his friend, but Burns was well enough one afternoon to visit Ruthwell Manse, where he took tea with the minister. The Reverend Craig and his daughter Agnes made him very welcome. Oddly enough, Craig was Nancy McLehose's maiden name. A contemporary account recalls:

His altered appearance excited much silent sympathy; and the evening being beautiful, and the sun shining brightly through the casement, Miss Craig was afraid the light might be too much for him, and rose with the view of letting down the window-blinds. Burns immediately guessed what she meant; and, regarding the young lady with a look of great benignity, said: 'Thank you, my dear, for your kind attention; but oh, let him shine: he will not shine long for me!

He spent much of the time writing letters. To James Armour in Mauchline (A7) he wrote –

My wife thinks she can reckon upon a fortnight...so it is ten thousand chances to one I shall not be within a dozen miles of her when her time comes...I have now been a week at the salt water, and though I think I may have got some good by it, yet I have some secret fears that this business will be dangerous, if not fatal.

He also wrote to his cousin, James Burness in Montrose, telling him of his fear of the haberdasher's writ and dread of jail. This fear was entirely unwarranted and without reason.

Williamson wasn't pursuing Burns. He had merely rendered his account, but in the state Burns was in, it reduced him to panic, hence his frantic tone –

> Will you be so good as to accommodate me, & that by return of post, with ten pounds? Oh James, if you did but know the pride of my heart, you would feel doubly for me! Alas! I am not used to beg...

His cousin sent the money by return.

And to George Thomson on 12 July 1796, enclosing his last song –

> After all my boasted independence, curst necessity compels me to implore you to send five pounds – a cruel haberdasher to whom I owe an account [for his Volunteers uniform and hat] taking it into his head that I am dying, has commenced a process, and will infallibly put me into jail – Do, for God's sake, send me that sum, and send it by return of post...upon returning health, I hereby promise and engage to furnish you with five pound's worth of the neatest song-genius you have seen...

Thomson sent the money at once.

Burns returned to Dumfries in a small spring cart on 18 July and went straight to his bed. His condition rapidly worsened as Jean's time drew nearer. Burns got desperate and wrote again to Armour – 'Do for Heaven's sake, send Mrs Armour immediately... my strength is so gone that the disorder will prove fatal to me.' News spread quickly through Dumfries that Burns was dying and crowds began to gather at his door. Visitors came all the time to his bedside and Burns, though weak, had still a word for them. To Dr Maxwell he said, 'What has brought you here? I am but a poor crow, and not worth the picking. I haven't feathers enough to carry me to my grave.' Then, pointing to his pistols, he asked the doctor to take them as Burns could not leave them in better hands. This also served as payment for his doctor's bills and both men knew it. When one of his brother-Volunteers called, he told him wryly, 'John, don't let the awkward squad fire over me!' Gradually he went into a delirium till, just after five o'clock in the morning of 21 July, as his children stood round the bedside, he suddenly rose up, called out 'Maxwell! McMurdo! Syme! Will none of you relieve me?' Then he slumped forward. Robert Burns was dead.

In the next room, Jean cried out and people thought it was the beginning of her labour, but it wasn't. While the crowds in the street outside watched his door, the final curtain came down on the life of Robert Burns, Poet – the curtain of an upstairs bedroom window. As the blind came down, one of the crowd was heard to mutter, 'Who'll be oor poet noo?'

Interestingly, the bank drafts for the money sent by James Burness, George Thomson and James Clarke, which had cost him so much to ask for, still lay uncashed on his table. Syme and Maxwell arranged the funeral for the 25th, and the remains of Burns, now clad in the contentious Volunteers uniform, lay in state at the town hall. Only Gilbert came down from Mauchline to represent the family. The body was then moved, in the solemnity of a great procession of a full-scale military funeral, to St Michael's Kirkyard where he was laid to rest. As the cortege moved to the solemn drumbeat through the streets, Jean gave birth to another son. She called him Maxwell, as her husband had requested.

The Dumfries Royal Volunteers *did* fire a salute over the grave – and nearly killed the minister. I am sure that somewhere 'abune them a' Robert Burns was laughing his head off. The Burns trail had finally come to its incongruous end in a puff of musket smoke.

Postscript

For thus the royal mandate ran
Since first the human race began
The honest, social, friendly man,
What e're he be,
'Tis he fulfils great Nature's plan
And none but he.

IN THE END WE MUST come back to Burns himself. We see now that
he went through five stages in his particular journey. In the first he
was introduced to books at Alloway (A1); in the second, at
Lochlea, to girls and poetry; in the third, at Edinburgh, to society
and fame; in the fourth, at Ellisland, to the theatre and the needs
of the family; and finally, at Dumfries, to song and the awareness
of his own posterity. His tours, in a sense, linked these various life
phases. While he was on the ostensible errand of merely vacation-
ing, he was also at the business of selling his books and the much
more serious business of selling himself. Which is why his propen-
sities as a play-actor and performer were so much to the fore at
these times. He loved being famous, being on show, and he rev-
elled in the applause. And why not? He was young, attractive,
articulate and charming. He was made to be admired, and he must
not be blamed too much for enjoying it.

If there's another world, he lives in bliss,
If not, he made the best of this.

He loved life but was given too little of it. But into those tight
37 years he compressed a life of such artistic vitality and energy
that it more than compensates for the brief span he was given in
which to do all that he had to do. Without ever leaving his own
country, except for the briefest of excursions into South Britain, he
has become universal. Without straining for a word outside his
own 'guid Scots tongue', he has spoken to all ages. It is pretty
remarkable really. The miracle was not that he wrote so well, but

that, given the conditions of his early life, he wrote at all. And, at the last, even in the short span he was given, he knew he had done enough. Robert Burns, as we have seen, could be all things to all men, but in his day he was always himself. That was a good part of his continual difficulties.

However, it is necessary to see him first as a man of his time, which was the second half of the 18th century. It was an extraordinary time of change in Scotland, culturally as well as politically, and over it all hung the Augustan mantle of Neo-classicism, the revolution of the mind which was called the Enlightenment. This affected Burns initially through John Murdoch, the Anglophile, who could not help but pass on the patrician stance in literature, which was the only one he knew. Burns, however, was sturdier mentally than Murdoch and somehow or other held on to his essential Scottishness by his own reading and by the influence of all those around him as he grew up. He, in fact, had the best of both worlds – the enlightening works of contemporary literature as Murdoch saw them, and the songs and stories of his mother and the common people which nourished the other side of the artist in him. The pincer effect of these two cultures, the written and the spoken, made his the unique voice it became.

He was, at root level, the 'satirist and singer of the parish' telling of ordinary things in unordinary ways, so that a mouse, a daisy, a louse become metaphors for a larger world. They offer a unique insight into the foibles of man and his society as seen by a remarkable young man in a remote, rural situation. That is the first thing about his genius that is significant – that he was so young when he did his finest work. As has been shown, most of his life's work was the product of a few early years. Yet, even then, he could speak with all the wisdom of the ages in some of his verse, with a shrewd insight, and above all with truth and humour, love and understanding. He had an encompassing compassion for every living thing from wounded hares to bullied peasantry and he carried their cases into his verse. This regard for all things is the theme that underpins his work.

In a way, one is almost glad he received no real patronage in his lifetime, although he was much assisted by the help he got from such as Glencairn and from contacts made through his Freemasonary. He never came under any fashionable pressures, because by the time they might have been applied, his work was done. Had he written entirely in English, for instance, in order to ingratiate himself with possible patrons, he would have been quite forgotten today. Thankfully, he held to his own muse. So he survives. This muse was anything but untutored, no matter his arch protestations about his station and the drivel he talks in his dedications about being caught at the plough. No man worked harder to get away from the plough. His claims to be untaught are just ruses to catch attention. They succeeded as we now know – perhaps too well. Like all geniuses, he knew he was good. He needed that certainty to do what he had to do. This is what gave him the courage to walk straight off the rigs and across a drawing-room carpet. He had something to say and, by God, he was going to say it.

In a sense, he was a watershed in himself. On the one hand, he was the culminating expression of the past, and on the other, a pointer towards the new romanticism and the ideas of personal freedom and equality that grew out of the revolutionary times. This Janus-like quality, being able to look forward and backward at the same time, is what typifies the artistic greats. They can always find the universal in the particular, the timeless in the ephemeral, and the meaningful in the absurd. Burns showed this in every line he wrote, which is why we still need his particular genius today. As mere mortals, we are all in constant need of reassurance. That's par for the course in our continuing human situation. In the two hundred and more years since his death, the world has gone on more or less as it has always done. The merry-go-round keeps turning, but things remain generally the same. Homo sapiens is constant whatever garb he wears. The essential man remains. He is greedy, glorious, frightened, valorous, pompous and modest all at once – and always looking for self-justification. We must look rather pitiable really, crawling the earth like ants, but then one of us suddenly rears up like a magnificent giant and reveals all the God that is in us. Burns was such a one. So are all artists. The artist is the God-watcher in man, hinting at the bigger things, the greater truths, which is why artistic fellow-mortals of quality, such as Burns, have been able, by their work, to provide this glimpse, in some measure, from generation to generation. Whether it be a splash of colour on canvas, a chord resounding in a concert hall, or words jumping out of the page, we are at one in a moment with the makers of these moments. Nothing artistic comes out of thin air, it has to be worked at, and when it works it makes us realise our humanity.

That is why good work lasts. We can read Burns today and feel something of what he felt in his own day. His best lines ring out with their own authenticity as if they have sprung from the very soil. We read him and become him as he becomes part of us. He speaks to all of us directly through the simplest of his lines. This is the real legacy of Robert Burns. This is his true immortality. It's certainly not due to Burns Suppers.

> *Ye Pow'rs wha mak Mankind your care*
> *And dish them oot their bill o' fare,*
> *Auld Scotland wants nae skinking ware*
> *That jaups in luggies;*
> *But, if ye wish her gratefu' prayer,*
> *Gie her a haggis!*

It is unfortunate that the modern image of Robert Burns is inextricably linked with haggis and the cult of the Burns Supper. When one thinks of the touching simplicity of the first, spontaneous gathering of Burns's admirers at Alloway (A1) in 1801 when nine men met to have sheep's heid and haggis and talk about him fondly, and then contrast that with the vast gatherings of corporate interests in five-star hotels brought together solely to drink the sponsor dry, one can only weep for the young man whose name and fame have been brought to such a travesty of the original intention. The Burns Supper of today is more Harry Lauder land than Burns country.

The average Burns Supper has little to do with the Burns these pages have tried to convey. His basic message – that the honest man is 'abune them a', and that 'man to man' should be brothers, and that 'the sweetest hours' are spent among the lassies – seems to have been misplaced in modern times, at least as far as the kilt-strewn Burns Supper is concerned. The modern format traduces the often-troubled young man. This most complicated of minds is little known to Burns revellers. They prefer their Rabbie with his breeches down. Why don't they just stick a paper hat on the Nasmyth portrait and be done with it?

Of course there are the serious students and the genuine Burns lovers who know and respect the works and the man, but their voice is little heard above the noise of unsteady feet going to and from the men's room. Nevertheless, all over the world, each January, whether in sun or snow, there are quiet gatherings where the essence of Burns is still evident, where people have taken the time to think about the man and be grateful for him. Many good people have worked tirelessly over the years to bring Burns to people through these annual gatherings and good luck to them. The real Burnsians deserve the reward of their sincere efforts in hearing a good 'Immortal Memory' proposed quietly and thoughtfully or a Burns song well sung without a microphone, but, oh dear, preserve us from the jumbo jamboree that tramples recklessly over what some of us still think of as hallowed ground.

Since its inception in 1885, the Burns Federation has done sterling work for Burns in every country around the globe, and during that time it has amassed a treasure-trove of Burns scholarship and experience in a hundred years of Burns Chronicles. Now, in the age of the Internet and electronic storage, it should be brought forward to a modern interpretation. It is a wonderful opportunity to start again, to create something new, something more appropriate to our times and to the status of the man we all seek to honour. The Burns Trail urgently needs to find a new direction.

Historically speaking, the Burns Country is a Concorde wing shape that links Dumfries (A23), Ayr (A2), Kilmarnock (A8) and Edinburgh. Topographically, this outline is extended north to Inverness (D20) and Aberdeen (D32) and south to Newcastle (C28) and Carlise (C32) to give us the complete extent of Burns's peregrinations in his lifetime, but essentially Burns belongs to the four places mentioned. Each carries something of Burns that relates to its own environment, but unfortunately, they also repeat each other, and even compete with each other. Some have artefacts and material in their possession that would be better set in any one of the other three places. Some inter-loans should be discussed per-

Burns Plaque, former Cross Keys Inn, Falkirk

haps. So I have a dream, a long hope, that the Burns managers in each centre might consider.

It is this – that state-of-the-art information centres be built or enlarged from what already exists to house the particular aspect of Burns appropriate to that place. For instance, in Ayr (A2), his birth-

place, every particle of information relating to Burns the Man, his family, the farms, his friends, would be tabulated and illustrated. Ayr, both town and county, would recognise the Patriot and Man of the land. Its centre would celebrate his love of Nature and all living things. Kilmarnock (A8) would honour Burns the

The Auld Kirk, Ayr

Wordsmith. Here should be seen every word he ever wrote and every comment written about him. This is Kilamrnock as the Robert Burns Mind Centre, and it ought to be in the charge of a new and streamlined Burns Federation with a full-time, professional

executive staff boasting every facility to do him proud. In Dumfries (A23), a similar centre would relate to Burns as Song-Maker and a Man of Scottish Music. He deserves further study under this heading, for he was a much under-rated musicologist. Such a centre would focus on Scottish music from a Burns point of view. Edinburgh, for its part, could concentrate on Burns the Internationalist and Poet of the World and might, for instance, house all the available translations of Burns into other languages.

These diverse centres would allow the world to know Robert Burns through varied aspects of his life and works in contemporary and exciting fashion. In this way, there would be no need for each of the recognised Burns places to repeat each other or vie for visitor interest. In this way the four sides of Burns – the Scot, the Poet, the Songwriter and the Internationalist would be served well and fully. Each centre would be complementary to the others and the four towns could thus splendidly justify their historical links with a Scottish genius.

Of course, such visions as these are wholly idealistic and utopian, but we must remember that Burns himself described his hopes to tour Scotland as 'wholly Utopian', but he did it. Hence this book. Perhaps such imaginings only belong in a book, but I feel there is an idea here for the future. Burns deserves the very best of Scottish know-how in whatever age. He needs an updated Burns Organisation, not a federation of social clubs. By all means, let us keep our pride in the Federation's achievement in keeping Burns's name to the fore, but that name is now in danger of being overtaken by the demands of the cybernetic age.

Burns has engaged the attention and respect of great minds since his lifetime. Let him continue to do so, in plays, concerts, musicals, novels and in the straightforward reading of his work, but he should be released from the gaudy glare of a once-a-year-spotlight. He can shine well enough in his own light. Similarly, his voice will be heard without a microphone being hurriedly set in place by a red-coated Toastmaster. It's time he was repatriated to the trousered Scottish dignity that is his right. Let's get back to the simple idea of people sitting down in friendship to eat and drink and remember him. Supper, after all, is supposed to a quiet meal at the end of the day. All that being said, and I sincerely believe, as one who loves Burns and has worked in Burns for most of my professional career, it is just as evident that there exists in Scotland a genuinely warm feeling towards Burns. He is still, with William Wallace and Robert Bruce, part of our iconic trinity. He has been woven into the very fabric of our national consciousness. Certainly, there are those who still think of him, if they ever think of him at all, as a drunken, womanising wastrel. Not all the dirt has been wiped from the deity and the misrepresentations persist as the myth continues to supercede the man.

Generally speaking, however, the average Scot knows well who Burns was and can quote something of his, even if it is only 'wee, sleekit, cowerin' tim'rous beastie' and the first four lines of *Auld Lang Syne*. The national aspect of Burns's image in Scotland is something he shares perhaps with Pushkin in Russia, Balzac in France and Mark Twain in America. It is more than a personal following, it is a people's identification with the writer, and he with it, and it is an indestructible bond. It is part of their posterity.

We can read him today as we would have read him in his own day. He is saying things that are timeless. That's his real immortality – his continuing aptness for the Scottish people. He is still appropriate to the common dream. He lives on in the hopes and aspirations of the common people, who, even today, still live in the belief that the best of their days are comin' – for a' that.

The Burns trail has its culmination in an imposing mausoleum in St Michael's Kirkyard in Dumfries. It is a splendid edifice, white and full of reverence, dominated by a carving and topped by a noble dome. Like his book of poetry, it was paid for by subscription, but it needs no guess as to which will survive the longer. The poems will be read and recited and the songs sung long after the masonry has crumbled and the carvings and statues have eroded. There never was a poet who has earned himself so many statues. There must be one in every city in the world. And who ever thought that words scribbled by a young Scottish farm labourer with a goosefeather at the end of a day's work would one day be translated into Esperanto; and that people all over the world would stand together, link arms and sing the world's anthem, *Auld Lang Syne*, one of his songs.

Burns Mausoleum

In this year of 1999, as I write these words, Scotland is reawakening to itself and to its own story and it needs its heroes. Burns has not been well served over the years by his idolators. Gradually, the people have claimed him again. He is back where he belongs, in the heart of Scotland, which is in the hearts of its ordinary people. And that's where the real Burns Trail begins and ends.

Bibliography

Selected Biographies

Daiches, David   *Robert Burns*, London, 1952.
                        Robert Burns and His World, 1971.
Ferguson, John de Lancey *Pride and Passion*, New York, 1939.
Gilfillan, George   *Life and Works*, Edinburgh, 1856.
Grimble, Ian   *Robert Burns*, London, 1986.
Hecht, Hans   *Robert Burns*, Heidleberg, 1919
                        (Translated Jane Lymburn, 1936).
Henley, William Ernest *The Centenary Burns*, 1896/97.
Lindsay, John Maurice   *The Ranting Dog*, 1938. (Robert Burns, 1954).
Mackay, James A.   *Burns*, Edinburgh, 1992.
McIntyre, Ian   *The Dirt and the Deity*, London, 1995.
Wright, Dudley   *Robert Burns and his Masonic Circle*,
                        Paisley, 1921/1929.

Burnsiana

Barke, James   Editor, *Complete Poems and Songs of Robert
                        Burns*, 1955, 1960, 1991 (Intro. by Editor)
                        1995 (Intro.by John Cairney). With Sydney
                        Goodsir Smith – Editor – *The Merry Muses of
                        Caledonia*. (Preface by J. De L. Ferguson),
                        London, 1965.
Bold, Alan   *A Burns Companion* (1991)
                        Robert Burns – a pictorial profile (1992)
                        *Rhymer Rab, an Anthology of the Prose and
                        Poetry of Burns* (1993).
Burns Chronicle   *Index of Articles 1892/1925 and 1926/45* by
                        J.C. Ewing.
Burns Encyclopaedia   London, 1959 (Edited by Maurice Lindsay).
Burnsiana   Alloway Publishing, 1988 (Compiled by
                        J.A. Mackay).
*Burns Information and
Quiz Book*   (Compiler Harold Thomas), Edinburgh, 1988.
Cairney, John   *A Moment White*, Glasgow, 1986.
                        The Man Who Played Robert Burns,

	Edinburgh, 1987.
	Robert Burns – A Brief Life (MS) – Auckland 1996.
Dictionary of National Biography	Vol 7 1886 (Entry by Sir Leslie Stephen).
Encyclopaedia Britannica	Vol 4 1876 (Entry by John Nichol).
Esslemont, Peter	*Brithers A'* – A Miscellany, Aberdeen, 1943.
Fisher, W.D.	*Burns and the Bible*, Glasgow, 1927.
Henley, W.E.	Editor (with T.F. Henderson) of *Centenary Edition of the Poetry of Robert Burns* (4 Vols) London, 1896.
Hepburn, Anthony	Editor, *Robert Burns – Poems and Selected Letters*, London, 1959. (Preface by Editor and Intro. by David Daiches.)
Hill, John C.	*The Love Songs & Heroines of Robert Burns*, London, 1961.
Hunter, Clark	*Let Burns Speak – An Edited Autobiography*, Paisley, 1961.
Irving, Gordon	*The Wit of Robert Burns*, London, 1972.
Keith, Christina	*The Russet Coat*, London, 1956.
Kinsley, James	*Burns Poems and Songs*, Oxford University Press, 1971.
Lamont-Brown, Raymond	Ed: *Commonplace Books of Robert Burns*, 1969.
	Robert Burns – Border Tour, Ipswich, 1972
	Robert Burns – Highland Tour, Ipswich, 1973
Low, Donald A.	*Critical Essays on Robert Burns*, London, 1975.
Mackay, James A.	*The Burns Federation 1885-1985*. Kilmarnock, 1985.
	The Complete Works, Alloway Publishing, 1986
	The Complete Letters of Robert Burns, Alloway, 1987.
	Burns-Lore of Dumfries and Galloway, Alloway, 1989.
	Burns A - Z , The Complete Word Finder, Dumfries, 1990.
	The Land o' Burns, Edinburgh, 1996.
McNaught, Duncan	*The Truth About Robert Burns*, Glasgow, 1921.
Montgomerie, William	Editor, *Robert Burns – Essays by Contemporary Authors*, Glasgow, 1947.
Munro, Archibald	*Burns and Highland Mary*, Edinburgh, 1896.

Murray, William James	'Robert Burns: the poet as liberationist'. Article in *The portrayal and condition of women in 18th-century literature*. Voltaire Collection. Section 18, session 4.
Pearl, Cyril	*Bawdy Burns – The Christian Rebel*, London, 1958.
Ross, John D.	*Burns' Clarinda*, Edinburgh, 1897.
Smith, Grant F.O.	Editor, *The Man Robert Burns,* Toronto, 1940.
Sprott, Gavin	Robert Burns: *Farmer*
Stevenson, R.L.	Essay – *Some Aspects of Robert Burns*
Stirling, James Hutchison	Editor, *Burns in Drama,* 1878, Murison Collection.
Stirling, L.M.	*Scotland's Sons* (Burns Chronicle, 1956) Mitchell Library, Glasgow.
Wallace, William	*Bicentenary Edition of Poetical Works of Robert Burns*, Edinburgh, 1958.
Westwood, Peter J.	*Jean Armour – Mrs Burns*, Dumfries, 1996
Wood, J. Maxwell	*Burns and the Riddell Family*, Dumfries, 1922.

Some other books published by **LUATH** PRESS

ON THE TRAIL OF

On the Trail of Robert Service

GW Lockhart

ISBN 0 946487 24 3 PBK £7.99

Robert Service is famed world-wide for his eye-witness verse-pictures of the Klondike goldrush. As a war poet, his work outsold Owen and Sassoon, and he went on to become the world's first million selling poet. In search of adventure and new experiences, he emigrated from Scotland to Canada in 1890 where he was caught up in the aftermath of the raging gold fever. His vivid dramatic verse bring to life the wild, larger than life characters of the gold rush Yukon, their bar-room brawls, their lust for gold, their trigger-happy gambles with life and love. 'The Shooting of Dan McGrew' is perhaps his most famous poem:

A bunch of the boys were whooping it up
in the Malamute saloon;
The kid that handles the music box was
hitting a ragtime tune;
Back of the bar in a solo game, sat
Dangerous Dan McGrew,
And watching his luck was his light
o'love, the lady that's known as Lou.

His storytelling powers have brought Robert Service enduring fame, particularly in North America and Scotland where he is something of a cult figure.

Starting in Scotland, *On the Trail of Robert Service* follows Service as he wanders through British Columbia, Oregon, California, Mexico, Cuba, Tahiti, Russia, Turkey and the Balkans, finally 'settling' in France.

This revised edition includes an expanded selection of illustrations of scenes from the Klondike as well as several photographs from the family of Robert Service on his travels around the world.

Wallace Lockhart, an expert on Scottish traditional folk music and dance, is the author of *Highland Balls & Village Halls* and *Fiddles & Folk*. His relish for a well-told tale in popular vernacular led him to fall in love with the verse of Robert Service and write his biography.

'*A fitting tribute to a remarkable man - a bank clerk who wanted to become a cowboy. It is hard to imagine a bank clerk writing such lines as:*

A bunch of boys were whooping it up...
The income from his writing actually exceeded his bank salary by a factor of five and he resigned to pursue a full time writing career.'
Charles Munn,

THE SCOTTISH BANKER

'*Robert Service claimed he wrote for those who wouldnit be seen dead reading poetry. His was an almost unbelievably mobile life... Lockhart hangs on breathlessly, enthusiastically unearthing clues to the poet's life.*' Ruth Thomas,

SCOTTISH BOOK COLLECTOR

'*This enthralling biography will delight Service lovers in both the Old World and the New.*' Marilyn Wright,

SCOTS INDEPENDENT

On the Trail of William Wallace

David R. Ross

ISBN 0 946487 47 2 PBK £7.99

How close to reality was *Braveheart*?

Where was Wallace actually born?

What was the relationship between Wallace and Bruce?

Are there any surviving eye-witness accounts of Wallace?

How does Wallace influence the psyche of today's Scots?

On the Trail of William Wallace offers a refreshing insight into the life and heritage of the great Scots hero whose proud story is at the very heart of what it means to be Scottish. Not concentrating simply on the hard historical facts of Wallace's life, the book also takes into account the real significance of Wallace and his effect on the ordinary Scot through the ages, manifested in the many sites where his memory is marked.

In trying to piece together the jigsaw of the reality of Wallace's life, David Ross weaves a subtle flow of new information with his own observations. His engaging, thoughtful and at times amusing narrative reads with the ease of a historical novel, complete with all the intrigue, treachery and romance required to hold the attention of the casual reader and still entice the more knowledgable historian.

74 places to visit in Scotland and the north of England

One general map and 3 location maps

Stirling and Falkirk battle plans

Wallace's route through London

Chapter on Wallace connections in North America and elsewhere

Reproductions of rarely seen illustrations

On the Trail of William Wallace will be enjoyed by anyone with an interest in Scotland, from the passing tourist to the most fervent nationalist. It is an encyclopaedia-cum-guide book, literally stuffed with fascinating titbits not usually on offer in the conventional history book.

David Ross is organiser of and historical adviser to the Society of William Wallace.

'Historians seem to think all there is to be known about Wallace has already been uncovered. Mr Ross has proved that Wallace studies are in fact in their infancy.' ELSPETH KING, Director the the Stirling Smith Art Museum & Gallery, who annotated and introduced the recent Luath edition of Blind Harry's Wallace.

'Better the pen than the sword!'

RANDALL WALLACE, author of Braveheart, when asked by David Ross how it felt to be partly responsible for the freedom of a nation following the Devolution Referendum.

On the Trail of Robert the Bruce

David R. Ross

ISBN 0 946487 52 9 PBK £7.99

On the Trail of Robert the Bruce charts the story of Scotland's hero-king from his boyhood, through his days of indecision as Scotland suffered under the English yoke, to his assumption of the crown exactly six months after the death of William Wallace. Here is the astonishing blow by blow account of how, against fearful odds, Bruce led the Scots to win their greatest ever victory. Bannockburn was not the end of the story. The war against English oppression lasted another fourteen years. Bruce lived just long enough to see his dreams of an independent Scotland come to fruition in 1328 with the signing of the Treaty of Edinburgh. The trail takes us to Bruce sites in Scotland, many of the little known and forgotten battle sites in northern England, and as far afield as the Bruce monuments in Andalusia and Jerusalem.

67 places to visit in Scotland and elsewhere.

One general map, 3 location maps and a map of Bruce-connected sites in Ireland.

Bannockburn battle plan.

Drawings and reproductions of rarely seen illustrations.

On the Trail of Robert the Bruce is not all blood and gore. It brings out the love and laughter, pain and passion of one of the great eras of Scottish history. Read it and you will understand why David Ross has never knowingly killed a spider in his life. Once again, he proves himself a master of the popular brand of hands-on history that made *On the Trail of William Wallace* so popular.

'David R. Ross is a proud patriot and unashamed romantic.'
SCOTLAND ON SUNDAY

'Robert the Bruce knew Scotland, knew every class of her people, as no man who ruled her before or since has done. It was he who asked of her a miracle - and she accomplished it.'
AGNES MUIR MACKENZIE

On the Trail of Mary Queen of Scots

J. Keith Cheetham
ISBN 0 946487 50 2 PBK £7.99

Life dealt Mary Queen of Scots love, intrigue, betrayal and tragedy in generous measure.

On the Trail of Mary Queen of Scots traces the major events in the turbulent life of the beautiful, enigmatic queen whose romantic reign and tragic destiny exerts an undimmed fascination over 400 years after her execution.

Places of interest to visit – 99 in Scotland, 35 in England and 29 in France.

One general map and 6 location maps.

Line drawings and illustrations.

Simplified family tree of the royal houses of Tudor and Stuart.

Key sites include:

Linlithgow Palace – Mary's birthplace, now a magnificent ruin

Stirling Castle – where, only nine months old, Mary was crowned Queen of Scotland

Notre Dame Cathedral – where, aged fifteen, she married the future king of France

The Palace of Holyroodhouse – Rizzio, one of Mary's closest advisers, was murdered here and some say his blood still stains the spot where he was stabbed to death

Sheffield Castle – where for fourteen years she languished as prisoner of her cousin, Queen Elizabeth I

Fotheringhay – here Mary finally met her death on the executioner's block.

On the Trail of Mary Queen of Scots is for everyone interested in the life of perhaps the most romantic figure in Scotland's history; a thorough guide to places connected with Mary, it is also a guide to the complexities of her personal and public life.

'In my end is my beginning'
MARY QUEEN OF SCOTS

'...the woman behaves like the Whore of Babylon' JOHN KNOX

POETRY

Poems to be read aloud

Collected and with an introduction by Tom Atkinson
ISBN 0 946487 00 6 PBK £5.00

This personal collection of doggerel and verse ranging from the tear-jerking *Green Eye of the Yellow God* to the rarely printed, bawdy *Eskimo Nell* has a lively cult following. Much borrowed and rarely returned, this is a book for reading aloud in very good company, preferably after a dram or twa. You are guaranteed a warm welcome if you arrive at a gathering with this little volume in your pocket.

'This little book is an attempt to stem the great rushing tide of canned entertainment. A hopeless attempt of course. There is poetry of very high order here, but there is also some fearful doggerel. But that is the way of things. No literary axe is being ground.

Of course some of the items in this book are poetic drivel, if read as poems. But that is not the point. They all spring to life when they are read aloud. It is the combination of the poem with your voice, with all the art and craft you can muster, that produces the finished product and effect you seek.

You don't have to learn the poems. Why clutter up your mind with rubbish? Of course, it is a poorly furnished mind that doesn't carry a fair stock of poetry, but surely the poems to be remembered and savoured in secret, when in love, or ill, or sad, are not the ones you want to share with an audience.

So go ahead, clear your throat and transfix all talkers with a stern eye, then let rip!'
TOM ATKINSON

Blind Harry's Wallace

William Hamilton of Gilbertfield
Introduced by Elspeth King
Illustrations by Dwain Kirby
ISBN 0 946487 43 X HBK £15.00
ISBN 0 946487 33 2 PBK £8.99
The original story of the real braveheart, Sir William Wallace. Racy, blood on every page, violently anglophobic, grossly embellished, vulgar and disgusting, clumsy and stilted, a literary failure, a great epic.

Whatever the verdict on BLIND HARRY, this is the book which has done more than any other to frame the notion of Scotland's national identity. Despite its numerous 'historical inaccuracies', it remains the principal source for what we now know about the life of Wallace.

The novel and film *Braveheart* were based on the 1722 Hamilton edition of this epic poem. Burns, Wordsworth, Byron and others were greatly influenced by this version 'wherein the old obsolete words are rendered more intelligible', which is said to be the book, next to the Bible, most commonly found in Scottish households in the eighteenth century. Burns even admits to having 'borrowed... a couplet worthy of Homer' directly from Hamilton's version of BLIND HARRY to include in *Scots wha hae*.

'Builder of the literary foundations of a national hero-cult in a free and powerful country'.
ALEXANDER STODDART, sculptor

'A true bard of the people'
TOM SCOTT, THE PENGUIN BOOK OF SCOTTISH VERSE, on Blind Harry.

'A more inventive writer than Shakespeare'
RANDALL WALLACE

'The story of Wallace poured a Scottish prejudice in my veins which will boil along until the floodgates of life shut in eternal rest'.
ROBERT BURNS

'Hamilton's couplets are not the best poetry you will ever read, but they rattle along at a fair pace. In re-issuing this work, the publishers have re-opened the spring from which most of our conceptions of the Wallace legend come'.
SCOTLAND ON SUNDAY

'The return of Blind Harry's Wallace, a man who makes Mel look like a wimp'.
THE SCOTSMAN

LUATH GUIDES TO SCOTLAND

Mull and Iona: Highways and Byways
Peter Macnab
ISBN 0 946487 58 8 PBK £4.95

SouthWest Scotland
Tom Atkinson
ISBN 0 946487 04 9 PBK £4.95

The West Highlands: The Lonely Lands
Tom Atkinson
ISBN 0 946487 56 1 PBK £4.95

The Northern Highlands: The Empty Lands
Tom Atkinson
ISBN 0 946487 55 3 PBK £4.95

The North West Highlands: Roads to the Isles
Tom Atkinson
ISBN 0 946487 54 5 PBK £4.95

NATURAL SCOTLAND

Wild Scotland: the essential guide to finding the best of natural Scotland
James McCarthy
Photography by Laurie Campbell
ISBN 0 946487 37 5 PBK £7.50

Scotland Land and People An Inhabited Solitude
James McCarthy
ISBN 0 946487 57 X PBK £7.99

'Nothing but Heather!'
Gerry Cambridge
ISBN 0 946487 49 9 PBK £15.00

Rum: Nature's Island
Magnus Magnusson
ISBN 0 946487 32 4 PBK £7.95

The Highland Geology Trail
John L Roberts
ISBN 0 946487 36 7 PBK £4.99

Red Sky at Night
John Barrington
ISBN 0 946487 60 X PBK £8.99

Listen to the Trees
Don MacCaskill
ISBN 0 946487 65 0 PBK £9.99

FOLKLORE

Tall Tales from an Island
Peter Macnab
ISBN 0 946487 07 3 PBK £8.99

The Supernatural Highlands
Francis Thompson
ISBN 0 946487 31 6 PBK £8.99

Scotland: Myth, Legend and Folklore
Stuart McHardy
ISBN: 0 946487 69 3 PBK 7.99

Tales from the North Coast
Alan Temperley
ISBN 0 946487 18 9 PBK £8.99

NEW SCOTLAND

**Scotland - Land and Power
the agenda for land reform**
Andy Wightman
foreword by Lesley Riddoch
ISBN 0 946487 70 7 PBK £5.00

**Notes from the North
incorporating a Brief History of the
Scots and the English**
Emma Wood
ISBN 0 946487 46 4 PBK £8.99

Old Scotland New Scotland
Jeff Fallow
ISBN 0 946487 40 5 PBK £6.99

WALK WITH LUATH

Mountain Days & Bothy Nights
Dave Brown and Ian Mitchell
ISBN 0 946487 15 4 PBK £7.50

The Joy of Hillwalking
Ralph Storer
ISBN 0 946487 28 6 PBK £7.50

Scotland's Mountains before the Mountaineers
Ian Mitchell
ISBN 0 946487 39 1 PBK £9.99

LUATH WALKING GUIDES

Walks in the Cairngorms
Ernest Cross
ISBN 0 946487 09 X PBK £4.95

Short Walks in the Cairngorms
Ernest Cross
ISBN 0 946487 23 5 PBK £4.95

SPORT

**Over the Top with the Tartan
Army (Active Service 1992-97)**
Andrew McArthur
ISBN 0 946487 45 6 PBK £7.99

Ski & Snowboard Scotland
Hilary Parke
ISBN 0 946487 35 9 PBK £6.99

SOCIAL HISTORY

The Crofting Years
Francis Thompson
ISBN 0 946487 06 5 PBK £6.95

A Word for Scotland
Jack Campbell
with a foreword by Magnus Magnusson
ISBN 0 946487 48 0 PBK £12.99

**Notes from the North
incorporating a Brief History of the
Scots and the English**
Emma Wood
ISBN 0 946487 46 4 PBK £8.99

Shale Voices
Alistair Findlay
foreword by Tam Dalyell MP
ISBN 0 946487 78 2 HBK £17.99
ISBN 0 946487 63 4 PBK £10.99

MUSIC AND DANCE

Highland Balls and Village Halls
GW Lockhart
ISBN 0 946487 12 X PBK £6.95

**Fiddles & Folk: a celebration of the
re-emergence of Scotland's musical
heritage**
GW Lockhart
ISBN 0 946487 38 3 PBK £7.95

FICTION

The Bannockburn Years
William Scott
ISBN 0 946487 34 0 PBK £7.95

Grave Robbers
Robin Mitchell
ISBN 0 946487 72 3 PBK £7.99

The Great Melnikov
Hugh MacLachlan
ISBN 0 946487 42 1 PBK £7.95

BIOGRAPHY

**Tobermory Teuchter: a first-hand
account of life on Mull in the early
years of the 20th century**
Peter Macnab
ISBN 0 946487 41 3 PBK £7.99

Bare Feet and Tackety Boots
Archie Cameron
ISBN 0 946487 17 0 PBK £7.95

Come Dungeons Dark
John Taylor Caldwell
ISBN 0 946487 19 7 PBK £6.95

Luath Press Limited
committed to publishing well written books worth reading

LUATH PRESS takes its name from Robert Burns, whose little collie Luath (*Gael.*, swift or nimble) tripped up Jean Armour at a wedding and gave him the chance to speak to the woman who was to be his wife and the abiding love of his life. Burns called one of *The Twa Dogs* Luath after Cuchullin's hunting dog in *Ossian's Fingal*. Luath Press grew up in the heart of Burns country, and now resides a few steps up the road from Burns' first lodgings in Edinburgh's Royal Mile.

Luath offers you distinctive writing with a hint of unexpected pleasures.

Most UK bookshops either carry our books in stock or can order them for you. To order direct from us, please send a £sterling cheque, postal order, international money order or your credit card details (number, address of cardholder and expiry date) to us at the address below. Please add post and packing as follows: UK – £1.00 per delivery address; overseas surface mail – £2.50 per delivery address; overseas airmail – £3.50 for the first book to each delivery address, plus £1.00 for each additional book by airmail to the same address. If your order is a gift, we will happily enclose your card or message at no extra charge.

ILLUSTRATION: IAN KELLAS

Luath Press Limited
543/2 Castlehill
The Royal Mile
Edinburgh EH1 2ND
Telephone: 0131 225 4326 (24 hours)
Fax: 0131 225 4324
email: gavin.macdougall@luath.co.uk
Website: www.luath.co.uk